GROUND FORCE
CONTAINER GARDENING

Charlie Dimmock

BBC

SAFETY WARNING

Some of the projects in this book involve the use of electrical appliances. Always be aware that using tools incorrectly or without due care can have fatal results and always read the instructions before you start. Paints, spray paints and varnishes are also used in many of the projects. These should be stored out of the reach of children. Always follow the manufacturer's advice when applying them and work out of doors or in a well-ventilated area. This book includes water garden projects and it should be observed that children can drown in very shallow depths of water and must not be left unsupervised near a water feature. It should also be noted that many garden plants are potentially poisonous. Always read plant labels carefully before planting and make sure that children and pets do not put poisonous plants in their mouths. The publishers and the author cannot accept responsibility or liability for accidents incurred as a result of the construction of any of the projects described in this book.

This book is published to accompany the television series entitled *Ground Force*, which was first broadcast in 1997. The series is produced by Endemol UK Productions for BBC Television.
Executive Producer: Carol Haslam
Producer/director: John Thornicroft

Published by BBC Worldwide Limited, Woodlands, 80 Wood Lane, London W12 0TT

First published 2002
Main introduction and seasonal introductions
© BBC Worldwide Limited, 2002
Text and all photographs (except those indicated in the picture credits on page 126) © GE Fabbri Ltd, 2000
The moral right of the author has been asserted.

ISBN 0 563 48809 3

Commissioning editor: Nicky Copeland
Editorial and design: Tucker Slingsby Ltd
Copy editor: Sally Harding
Designer: Robert Mathias

Set in Gill sans serif and Formata
Printed and bound in France by Imprimerie Pollina s.a.
Colour separations by Studio One, London and Kestrel Digital Colour Ltd, Chelmsford, Essex
Cover printed by Imprimerie Pollina s.a.

endemol u.k.

Contents

Introduction

Do you know what I find the most satisfying part of working on a garden for *Ground Force*? It's after the patio has been laid, the pond dug and the plants are settled into their beds, when I can concentrate on the finishing touches that bring the garden to life and make it unique. And often it's the choice, position and planting of the containers that makes a garden look really special. I love hunting for attractive and unusual containers, choosing plants to complement them and planting them up to make a perfect partnership. Then there's the fun of finding the best spot for each container – on a patio, path or wall – where it will catch the eye and add interest and colour to the garden. Container gardening is so easy and instant it's almost too good to be true. If you haven't been bitten by the bug yet you're missing out on a real treat!

For many people, containers are a lot more than the final details. If you have a tiny backyard, balcony or roof garden, then pots, window boxes and baskets may be the only way to create a garden. And the result can look just as stunning as acres of shrub borders and lawns. You can even have a pond in a pot!

With a bit of forward planning it's not difficult to plant up your containers so that you have flowers to greet you every day of the year. With this in mind, I've planned arrangements for all four seasons. To get you started I've included lots of pots that are really simple to plant up and arrange. Once you're hooked on container gardening, you'll want to try the others that are a little more demanding. So I've put in some of those too! You'll find ideas for imaginative and colourful plantings using bright annuals, climbers in pots, tasty salad crops, towers of herbs, instant topiary, winter foliage and berry arrangements – and, of course, I just had to have a couple of miniature water gardens!

I would be misleading you if I didn't say that to have good-looking containers you need to give them a bit of attention on a regular basis. You can't rely on natural rainfall to water pots, so regular watering is a major priority. But the rewards are worth the effort. And bear in mind you can install automatic irrigation systems or grow desert-style plants that will tolerate a bit of neglect.

I am sure you will find just the container style you are looking for in this book, whether it's modern architectural to complement your outdoor living space, cottage garden romance, oriental simplicity or even a taste of the tropics. There are step-by-step instructions for each arrangement, plus growing tips to guide you along. I've included hanging baskets, window boxes, formal urns, glazed and terracotta pots, wicker baskets – and none of the displays costs a fortune. With the basics under your belt, these projects will also be a source of ideas that you can adapt to your own taste. The possibilities are endless. Almost any plant will grow in a container and finding out what looks best where is half the fun!

Happy container gardening!

Getting started

Why containers?

The answer is simple, although a potted paradise takes a bit of effort to maintain, it's the quickest and simplest way to give your garden a facelift – if you haven't got the *Ground Force* team on call that is! A quick trip to the garden centre and you can brighten up your house with colourful window boxes, transform a boring patio into a flower-filled haven and create little oases of interest in neglected corners of your garden.

Your house can be dressed with window boxes and hanging baskets at ground-floor level or you can put them higher to frame upstairs windows with foliage and flowers – take care to fasten them securely. Two matching container displays either side of the gate or front door always looks spectacular as does a collection of containers marching down the front steps. And it's not just the look of your house that improves, the cherry-pie scent of heliotrope drifting in through an open window on a warm summer evening is a delight.

For practical reasons, many gardens are isolated from the house by a strip of concrete slabs. This is an area crying out for containers, which can be placed right up to the patio doors and windows. With potted plants indoors as well as out, the division between house and garden begins to melt away. Containers on the patio are especially valuable in winter. You can crowd everything together that looks pretty and arrange the pots where you can see them from indoors.

A large container filled with one spectacular plant or a display of colourful flowers makes a focal point which draws the eye. You can use this effect to add interest to a plain patch of lawn or to draw attention away from a boring bit of wall or less than perfect border. A big stone urn or terracotta planter is costly but should stay looking good for years.

Containers are also invaluable because they enable you to grow what you want – camellias, even though your garden soil contains lime; when you want – golden roses forced on in the greenhouse for a special

ORNAMENTAL GRASSES IN A SALT-GLAZED TERRACOTTA POT

anniversary; where you want – scented plants right next to your favourite seat. And with containers you can select styles of pots and plants ranging from oriental through to tropical, classical, formal, modern minimalist or cosy cottage garden.

THE VARIEGATED IVIES IN THESE CHUNKY TERRACOTTA POTS
WILL LOOK GOOD ALL YEAR ROUND, WHILE THE PETUNIAS IN
SOFT PINKS ADD SUMMER COLOUR

For the cook in the family, individual containers can
be a miniature allotment – even if you've only a balcony –
providing crisp salad leaves and sweet cherry tomatoes,
a strawberry farm, or a tower of fresh herbs next to the
kitchen door. If you've longed for a pond but only have
a postage stamp of a garden, you can create a water
garden in a pot – complete with water lilies.

The mobility of containers can be turned to your
advantage in a variety of ways. If you've only a balcony,
roof garden or tiny concrete yard, everything you grow
will have to be contained in planters and may even have
to arrive through a lift or narrow corridor. And, of course,
when you move house you can take your containers with
you – a point worth bearing in mind if you love gardening
but have to relocate regularly.

Although our winters do seem to be getting milder,
there are still borderline hardy plants like cordylines,
clipped bays and agaves that need to be overwintered in
a frost-free greenhouse, conservatory or protected
porch, especially in colder areas. If you grow them in
pots, they can be whisked inside in minutes.

I hope I have given you a sufficient number of reasons
to start a lifelong love of container gardening!

Choosing containers

When I'm sent out to shop for containers for one of the *Ground Force* gardens, it's a real treat because I'm spoilt for choice. Containers are now available from all over the world: nests of colourful bowls and tall square planters from Vietnam and China, brown mud pots from Thailand, pale terracotta jars and pans from Crete and Spain, classical designs with swags and cherubs from Italy, and antique oil jars from Morocco and Turkey. So that I don't get carried away, I always consider three things before buying – the style I want to create, the shape that will look best and the material I want to use.

TERRACOTTA

The vast majority of pots available are made from terracotta, though you may not realize it when they are finished off with beautifully coloured glazes that look good and usually make them more resistant to the frost. Faced with such a selection, I often plump for homemade terracotta. It may be more expensive, but with its carefully selected clays and high firing temperatures, many pots carry a 10- or even 20-year guarantee against frost damage.

The porous nature of terracotta makes it ideal for containers, allowing air to get through to the compost and the plants' roots, which then dry out more quickly, preventing waterlogging. If you are worried about killing plants by overwatering them, terracotta

could be for you. It also weathers to a wonderful mellow finish as deposits of algae and lime build up on the surface. Of course, it is brittle and can be heavy to move around, but its weight and stability will anchor a plant like a tall bamboo to the patio, even in strong winds, as long as you have not allowed the pot to dry out.

PLASTIC

Plastic containers are light and easy to carry around and weight may be an important factor if you are planning a roof garden or balcony display. Plastic pots have come a long way since the white urns that were seen on every patio in the '60s and are now made in a variety of styles including ones with a very convincing terracotta or stone finish. If you are after a really outsize container for a tree, plastic ones will almost certainly be the best value for money. After all, that's how nurseries grow their large specimen plants. Plastic troughs are also useful as a liner to extend the life of a wooden window box. Cheap plastic, however, becomes brittle after a few seasons if exposed to the sun.

WOOD

Wooden containers have a warmth and solidity that will always satisfy the eye. They are well insulated in the winter, a time when frost damage to roots can kill container plants.

THIS COURTYARD GARDEN WAS TRANSFORMED WHEN WE ADDED CONTAINERS FILLED WITH SHRUBS AND TREES, LIKE THIS *CORYLUS AVELLANA* 'CONTORTA'

With their ability to retain moisture, wooden containers are perfect for woodland plants like rhododendrons, camellias and Japanese maples. Look out for wooden half barrels which are large enough to keep even quite a big shrub happy. Versailles planters – those smart square tubs with knobs on the corners – are just the thing to frame a formal front door or arch. They can be painted in classic dark green or to echo the colour scheme of your house. Plant them with a matching pair of neatly clipped box or bay for a really traditional look.

FORMAL AND INFORMAL

A reconstituted stone urn, cast in a mould, is expensive, but when set up on a plinth, can provide the high spot of the garden. This material soon weathers to take on the patina of natural stone and looks best in formal settings. Lead has a similar air of sophistication, but is heavy and expensive. Again, however, there are some very clever fibreglass planters with a fake lead finish.

For an informal garden, I like simple terracotta pots, wicker baskets, and recycled junk. Containers made from tin baths and buckets and colanders are particular favourites of mine. When I'm looking for pots to place on decking, I go for more modern designs like Ali-Baba jars, square pots and hi-tech galvanized containers. With swaying grasses they look fabulous. Make sure, however, that whichever pot you choose, it has an opening wide enough for you to take the plant out for repotting.

ABOVE: A SILVERED POT REFLECTS BRILLIANT RED PELARGONIUMS

TOP LEFT: A PRETTY, PAINTED WOODEN TROUGH PLANTED WITH CYCLAMEN AND IVIES

LEFT: THIS TONING, BLUE-GLAZED POT FLANKS THE DIVIDE BETWEEN THE DECK AND PATIO

Decorating containers

On *Ground Force* we often get clues about the best style of container to choose by looking at the interior of the owner's house. And when it comes to colour – if you can't find a pot or planter just the right shade, follow the *Ground Force* way and paint it! Changing the colour of fences and walls creates a new dimension in a garden, and painting your pots can do the same. To create a colour scheme for your pots, you can simply pick up the colour of your house doors or window frames or go for the same shade as the fences and trellis. Or, for a more sophisticated finish, introduce both colour and pattern by sponging, stencilling or brushing the paint on to your containers. I love the hot, clashing patterns of Mexico, but take your pick from bold, geometric Art-Deco style, the sculptural, plant-inspired qualities of Japanese decoration or the simplicity of the North American Shaker style.

One of the most satisfying aspects of pot decorating is turning a plain pot into something really special. Not being the world's greatest artist, I find I often get the best results using inexpensive terracotta containers (but check out they are frost-proof) and painting them a single colour or with a simple stylized design. Old tin baths and buckets, which may look a little battered and dull, can also benefit from a facelift.

Decorated containers must be able to withstand the ravages of sun, rain and frost, so always use exterior products. Good DIY stores and garden centres stock a wide range of outdoor paints and many are clearly marked as suitable for pots. However, you can achieve a quite hard-wearing finish using a much wider range of paints, as long as you apply them over a primer and protect them with a couple of coats of clear matt varnish when the paint is completely dry.

Simple Shaker style

1 To transform a small tin bucket, first paint it inside and out with red oxide paint. Cut out a heart shape from a piece of stencil card to create a pattern in a Shaker style.

2 Attach the stencil to the container with masking tape. Dip a stencil brush in acrylic paint, dab off the excess, then stencil the heart on to the bucket with a dabbing motion.

3 Remove the stencil from the bucket with care so as not to smear the paint, then reuse it on another bucket. Planted up with aromatic herbs, these Shaker pots look simply stylish.

Plain colour

When painting bold horizontal or vertical stripes, I use masking tape to give really sharp lines. Don't apply it until the first colour is really dry or some of the original colour may show through when you peel off the tape. For simple shapes, I use a template. Other decorative finishes I like are verdigris, that subtle blue-green you see on old pieces of copper when they are left to weather outdoors, which can now be bought in kit form, and metallic paints that can make plastic look like stainless steel.

1 *For Mediterranean style, paint a narrow-necked jar a vivid blue colour. Cover an outdoor work surface with newspaper, then stand the pot inside a box before spraying. Wearing a protective mask, spray the outside and about 5cm (2in) down the inside with satin finish aerosol craft paint.*

FOR THIS *GROUND FORCE* GARDEN, WE USED ALUMINIUM PAINT TO TURN AN INEXPENSIVE PLASTIC POT INTO A STUNNING PLANTER FOR *GERANIUM MACRORRHIZUM* 'BEVAN'S VARIETY'

2 *Let the spray paint dry and apply a second coat if necessary. Two lightly sprayed coats are better than one thick one which may form drips. When the paint is completely dry, apply two coats of clear, matt polyurethane varnish.*

Preparing for planting

As with most day-to-day things you do – cooking a meal, putting up shelves, planting up a flower border – a bit of advance planning will not only get the job done in double-quick time, you will also enjoy doing it a lot more. We always have a shopping list when we start a *Ground Force* project. There is nothing more annoying than getting back on site with a vital piece of kit missing. There's no great mystique attached to container gardening. Much of it is pretty straightforward, but the most common mistakes are likely to be made through inadequate preparation. Take drainage for example. A surprising number of containers, usually ceramic pots and galvanized planters, are still sold without drainage holes. This is fine if you are using them as pot holders to prevent water escaping, for indoor use, perhaps, or to make a mini water feature, but very few plants like to be waterlogged or standing in water. The compost becomes stagnant and the roots die through lack of oxygen. (Incidentally, if the reverse is the case, and you want to turn a glazed pot with drainage holes into a pond, just line the container with plastic to make it watertight.)

The walls of metal containers are thin enough for you to be able to punch holes in the base with a hammer and nail, and I've had to do this many times when working on *Ground Force* gardens. If the container is especially thick, use an electric or battery-operated drill with a metal drilling bit. Ceramic and terracotta pots require a bit more care. You will need a masonry bit and protective gloves and goggles. Chips can fly off when drilling, so keep children and pets away from where you are working. Plastic containers usually come with half pierced holes in the base, so you only need to remove a thin layer of plastic.

Other pre-planting jobs include soaking new terracotta pots overnight in a tank of water to prevent them from drawing moisture out of the potting compost and treating wicker baskets with two or three coats of clear preservative or yacht varnish.

It may sound obvious, but unless you are really strong, or have Tommy to help you, set large pots and troughs in their final positions before adding plants and potting compost. After watering they will be very heavy to move. Flat-bottomed containers will benefit from being

KEEP YOUR POTS OFF THE GROUND BY STANDING THEM ON TERRACOTTA FEET, AVAILABLE IN PLAIN UNGLAZED OR GLAZED TO MATCH YOUR POT

USING A HAMMER AND NAIL TO PUNCH DRAINAGE HOLES IN A GALVANIZED METAL WASTEPAPER BIN IS SURPRISINGLY EASY. MAKE AT LEAST FIVE HOLES EVENLY SPACED OVER THE BASE

set up on pot feet to raise them off the ground. Not only do terracotta feet look good, they will aid drainage, make your pots easier to sweep around and stop worms from crawling in and blocking the holes.

If you want to sound like a professional, start calling the mixture you use to fill containers compost and not soil or worse still 'dirt'! It will earn you Brownie points at garden centres and ensure you get the growing medium you want. There are two main types of compost for containers: loam or soil-based compost; and soil-free compost, usually called multipurpose or potting compost, which is traditionally a blend of peat, sharp sand and slow-release fertilizer. Soil-based mixes are best for long-term planting – hardy shrubs and small trees for example. They retain food and moisture longer than soil-less types. Soil-free composts are light, clean to handle and ideal for seasonal displays. There are also mixtures of both kinds and peat-free, environmentally

friendly substitutes that contain shredded bark or coir (coconut fibre). You can also buy special mixes for plants with specific needs like alpines and cacti (with extra grit to improve the drainage). Buy ericaceous compost (lime-free) for acid-loving plants such as camellias. For hanging baskets look out for compost with water-retaining gel to increase its moisture-holding capacity.

When considering drainage to go inside the bottom of your container, choose either broken pieces of terracotta (known as crocks) or, most conveniently, broken up chunks of polystyrene which do not add to the weight of the container and are easily available. A layer of either material placed in the bottom of your container before adding the compost will help prevent plants from becoming waterlogged.

HIBISCUS SYRIACUS 'BLUE BIRD' IN A POT SETS OFF THIS SHELTERED SEATING AREA

Planting

Now for the exciting part, planting up your containers. In summer, a little time spent planting up in May and early June will provide months of colour only cut short by the first severe frost. What's more, in my own garden I can pick a pleasant sunny day, rather than having to work in the rain that seems to join in when we're working on the gardens to be televised! I really look forward to surrounding myself with an array of flowers and foliage, blending them together and giving them the best possible start. Generally speaking, I work to a theme – scent, single or two-tone colours, something to eat or flavour my meals – though this doesn't prevent me from growing several varieties in a single container.

Providing good drainage, as I mentioned on the previous page, is the first part of the operation. Lining the base of the container with drainage material will prevent wet compost clogging up the drainage hole or holes and the pot becoming waterlogged. Terracotta crocks work well and are a good way of using up broken flower pots, but chunks of polystyrene are light and often more accessible. I break up those carry-home shuttle trays you can get from garden centres that are used for slotting in

Planting lily bulbs

1 *For good drainage, add a few crocks then 5cm (2in) of gravel to a 36cm (14in) tall pot.*

2 *Add multipurpose compost up to half the depth of the pot.*

3 *Space out the lily bulbs on top of 2.5cm (1in) of horticultural grit.*

4 *Cover the lily bulbs with at least another 15cm (6in) of compost.*

your plant purchases. They're very effective and they're free! As a general rule, fill up about a quarter of the depth of the container with drainage material before adding the potting compost and plants.

What size of plant you buy depends on whether you want an arrangement that is 'instant' and looks good from day one, using more mature plants, or one that improves with age, which I prefer because it tends to look more natural. Of course, the more mature a plant the more expensive it will be. For a really big showy display, I like to mix together plants with contrasting shapes – tall upright plants in the centre or at the back surrounded by round bushy ones plus trailing plants around the outside to spill over and soften the edge of the pot. Bear in mind whether the container will be seen

from one side only, against a wall or fence for example, or from all sides as you walk round the garden.

Before putting the plants in, make sure they are all well watered: soak them in a bucket for up to an hour if they're really dry because it is almost impossible to water them this well once they are in containers. Then remove them carefully from their pots by turning them upside down and tapping the rim of the pot all round to loosen the compost and roots. Position the plant with the deepest rootball first, then add the smaller ones, leaving the finished compost level 2.5-5cm (1-2in) below the rim to allow for watering. To encourage plants at the edge to spill over the sides, angle them outwards a little. Finally, remove any compost from hairy leaves, such as those of petunias, with a hand-held water sprayer.

Arranging your plants

1 *First arrange the plants on the ground until you achieve the effect you like, bushy in the middle, trailers at the edge.*

2 *Remove them from their plastic pots and sink the pots in the compost as 'moulds' that match your planting pattern.*

3 *Take out the pots one by one, replacing them with the correct plant from your arrangement.*

4 *Top up with extra compost if required. Firm the plants in gently and level off the compost.*

Keeping containers looking good

The most inspiring container displays are grown by gardeners who have developed a real 'feel' for their plants and can tell at a glance when they are in need of water, food, a bigger pot or just a good tidy up. If you can play doctor to them, your plants will reward you with luxuriant growth. Professional growers achieve this by keeping their plants growing steadily throughout the seasons, so they never suffer from a check in growth by being starved or dried out. It's not rocket science, but I know from experience that having a few pieces of essential maintenance equipment to hand is one of the keys to success. A well-balanced, long-necked watering can turns watering from a chore to a pleasure. A fine rose on the end of the spout is ideal for soaking seedlings and plug plants without washing them away. As you find container gardening becoming more addictive, you'll soon have a patio crammed with pots. At this stage, a hose-end lance with an adjustable spray head will save you hours of watering. Some spray heads can be filled with blocks of feed that are diluted as you water, so you can water and feed at the same time, with no measuring.

The standard advice is to give container-grown plants a liquid feed every seven to ten days. If this seems too great a commitment, use push-in feed pellets that deliver

nutrients every time you water during the growing season. Water-retaining granules can also be mixed into the potting compost before planting up. They are especially useful for hanging baskets or window boxes on south-facing sills where they can make the difference between watering once rather than twice a day during hot, windy weather.

Just as having a dog to walk gets you up in the morning, so will having a mobile garden to tend. Get into a watering routine and you will make light work of it. Water in the morning or evening to reduce evaporation, and try to avoid splashing the leaves as this will cause them to scorch when exposed to strong sunlight. At holiday time, move your containers to a shady wall and stand them on special moisture-retentive capillary matting fed from a tin bath of water.

In the autumn, winter and spring months, plants need much less water, although it is surprising how a series of hard frosts can strip the moisture from the compost and this can only be replenished when the compost has thawed out. When the weather's particularly severe, it pays to gather your containers under a warm house wall where they will escape the worst of the weather.

Deadhead your plants regularly as soon as flowers fade. This will encourage a fresh flush of flower buds. Spent flowers left on the plant will usually inhibit further flower production, however, not all spent flowers need to be removed. Busy lizzies and those super-vigorous petunias carry on regardless. Some like marigolds can be snapped off. Others like pansies and nasturtiums can be nipped off by pinching them with your fingernails. Pointed scissors are ideal to snip off the long stems of faded sweet pea blooms. Secateurs are best for dahlias.

For bushy fuchsias and chrysanthemums with lots of blooms, pinch back the shoots regularly. Do this by simply nipping off the tips of shoots. At the end of summer, be ruthless and throw annuals past their best on to the compost heap. However, some plants sold for bedding, including pelargoniums, fuchsias and heliotrope, can be propagated from cuttings in late summer or dug up and overwintered in a frost-free greenhouse, porch or even the spare bedroom. They have the potential to get bigger and better every year.

If, like me, you hate using chemicals to control pests and diseases, you will have to keep a close eye on your containers, as early action will often nip the problem in the bud. Natural predators like ladybirds will eventually arrive to polish off those greenfly, but your plants may be half eaten in the meantime. The easiest option is to spray on a ready-mixed environmentally friendly treatment.

OPPOSITE FAR LEFT: FLOWERING GARLIC ON THIS DECK LOOKS STUNNING AGAINST A WATERY BACKDROP

OPPOSITE LEFT: ORIENTAL STYLE WITH A BONSAI TREE IN A RECONSTITUTED STONE CONTAINER

LEFT: THE GROUP OF CONTAINERS ON THIS DECK PROVIDES HEIGHT, COLOUR AND SEASONAL FLOWERS

Caring for permanent containers

Ask many gardeners what they want from their containers and the answer will be colour from January to December. That's a tall order! Lots of colourful flowers are easy to grow in late spring and summer, but difficult at other times of year. This is when permanent plants in containers come into their own. They fill the gaps between the more fleeting bulbs and summer flowers, and we often feature them in a *Ground Force* garden to give a backbone to the patio display. I think they also provide some of the most spectacular container sights, especially if you consider the sword-like leaves of cordylines, New Zealand flax and yuccas. These will be fine outdoors all year round in mild areas, although being contained in a pot will make them more susceptible to frosts, so in cold areas of the country it's safer to pop them under cover in a porch, conservatory or greenhouse for the worst of the winter. Alternatively, move them against a house wall and wrap garden fleece several times around their pots. This will prevent frost damage to the roots. Tree ferns will benefit from this treatment too. Encase their trunks in garden fleece and stuff some hay or straw into the crown of the plant at the top of the trunk where the fronds emerge.

A new pot for a large cordyline

1 *To remove a large pot-bound plant from its container, lay it on its side and ease out the rootball. This operation may need the strength of two people.*

2 *Without destroying the rootball, carefully tease out some of the roots that have circled around in the pot, so that they will grow into the new compost.*

3 *Sit your plant in the new pot on a layer of crocks and compost, then fill in around the rootball with more compost. Allow space below the rim for watering.*

The main job with plants grown permanently in containers is to move them on regularly into bigger pots before they become starved. This is called potting on. You may need to do this every year with vigorous varieties like the cordyline pictured here. Others, like rhododendrons and Japanese maples may be fine in the same pot for several years as long as they are fed and watered. So what are the distress signals that indicate your plant needs potting on? Yellowing leaves, lack of vigour and roots poking out through the drainage holes are sure signs. But the best way to find out is to knock your plant out of its pot and look for the tell-tale mass of tangled roots. If the pot is hard to remove, I use a soft-headed plastic mallet to knock the rim when it is on its side.

Soil-based composts are the most suitable for permanent subjects. Lime-hating varieties like rhododendrons and camellias will need an ericaceous compost to keep them healthy and growing well.

If after several years your plant is simply too big to pot on, either plant it out in the garden or scrape off the top few inches of compost with a hand fork and replace this with fresh compost. This may also be the only solution available to you if you have made the mistake of planting in a narrow-necked jar because it will be impossible to remove the plant without smashing it. Looking on the bright side, if you do have to resort to the hammer, you'll have a lifelong supply of crocks!

OPPOSITE: A BALL-SHAPED BOX IN A TERRACOTTA PLANTER WILL LOOK GOOD ALL YEAR ROUND

RIGHT: CORDYLINE WON'T NEED FEEDING FOR A COUPLE OF MONTHS AFTER REPLANTING. A SLOW-RELEASE FERTILIZER AFTER THAT WILL KEEP IT HEALTHY

4 *Remove any leaves that may have been damaged during potting on. Then add a layer of gravel on the surface to help to retain moisture.*

Spring

Spring containers

Spring is a magical time of year. Even professional gardeners like me and Alan never tire of seeing the earliest daffodils and tulips. And as the days get warmer there's the excitement of a new growing year ahead of us.

There is no excuse for empty patio containers and window boxes at this time of year. Garden centres are crammed with spring bulbs and bedding plants – and there's a lot more beside these: check out the shrubs, herbaceous perennials and even small trees; they will give your containers a more permanent framework, with seasonal plants added for instant colour. If you have the space, shrubs like camellias, daphnes and the dwarf *Magnolia stellata* that take centre stage in spring can be moved to a quieter corner of the garden after flowering, to be moved back into view next spring.

When I'm shopping for container shrubs for a *Ground Force* garden, I try to find ones that offer double value. Forsythia flowers, for instance, look stunning in the spring, but for the rest of the year, forsythia can be a bit boring. A camellia or pieris on the other hand has lovely glossy leaves all year round, as well as spring flowers.

I try to keep colour in my spring containers from early March to late May. You can do this with just bulbs, starting with the tiniest, like *Iris reticulata*, crocus and windflower (*Anemone blanda*), followed by dwarf daffodils and tulips and muscari. By late April and May, tall tulips steal the scene. My favourite combination is red tulips with blue muscari but if you are looking for less common bulbs, like parrot tulips or lilies, you'll need to plan ahead. The more unusual bulbs are unlikely to be on sale in pots in the spring, so you will need to buy bulbs and plant them the previous autumn.

Create different moods by your choice of plants – pots of single variety bulbs have a stylish simplicity, while bulbs mixed with spring bedding plants like forget-me-nots and pansies, and perennials like euphorbia and doronicums can look spectacular.

For containers to look good, remember to keep a sense of scale – tiny miniatures look comfortable in shallow bowls and pans, but are lost in a large urn. The same applies to the plants themselves. Giant-flowered pansies look great with tall daffodils; delicate violas with miniature daffodils.

MUST-HAVE PLANTS FOR SPRING CONTAINERS

Ajuga reptans 'Multicolor'
Anemone blanda
Camellia x *williamsii* 'Donation'
Choisya ternata 'Sundance'
Clematis alpina 'Columbine'
Daffodil 'Jetfire'
Dicentra 'Bacchanal'
Double daisies

Euphorbia x *martinii*
Grape hyacinth 'Blue Spike'
Helleborus orientalis
Hyacinth 'Delft Blue'
Pansy 'Imperial Antique Shades'
Pieris japonica 'Valley Valentine'

Primroses and polyanthus
Rhododendron 'Percy Wiseman'
Spiraea japonica 'Goldflame'
Tulip 'Peach Blossom'
Tulip 'Stresa'
Vinca minor 'Illumination'

Camellia display

Lime-hating camellias grow happily in containers, so if you have alkaline soil in your garden you needn't miss out on these fabulous flowers – just pop them in a spring display.

Camellias, with their exotic-looking flowers, bring a splash of much needed colour to the garden from early spring. But these plants hate lime, and they won't do well in many gardens, especially those with alkaline soil. Luckily, camellias and most other lime-hating plants thrive in containers, as long as you plant them in lime-free (ericaceous) potting compost.

To me, camellias look stunning simply planted on their own in a container, but with a clever choice of companion plants, you can create something really striking and original. The red flowers of Camellia 'Apollo', with their huge, bright yellow stamens, make an ideal focus for this red and yellow themed planting. Daffodils and primroses add the distinct flavour of spring and fill out the base of the display, while the evergreen shrubby honeysuckle 'Lemon Beauty' provides a gentle foliage background.

WHEN TO PLANT – **early to mid spring**

Planting your spring display

Choose the camellias for your arrangement very carefully and be imaginative with your choice of container. I found an old tin bath, which was perfect as I could fit quite a lot of plants into it, but you could make use of any container you have to hand, provided you make drainage holes in it before planting. Pick healthy, compact camellias with dark green foliage, some open flowers and plenty of fat buds that will carry on the show. If you buy daffodils and primroses in pots already in bloom, you can have instant colour.

Once planted, stand the container in sun or partial shade, but avoid east-facing sites (see page 30).

A perfect double act

For a simpler display, I like to pair a dwarf rhododendron with a single

camellia. My favourite rhododendron for a container is the dwarf 'Blue Diamond'. It makes a tight mound of foliage studded with hundreds of blue flowers and looks lovely sitting beneath a pink camellia. If I have to

choose just one camellia, I go for 'Donation'. It's dense and compact and never fails to cover itself in a glorious cloak of semi-double pink flowers each spring. Both plants enjoy a lightly shaded position.

1 *Turn your bath upside down and wedge it into a firm position. Wearing safety goggles and gloves, drill out a dozen drainage holes using an electric or battery-powered drill.*

2 *Assemble the plants listed in the You Will Need box – 'Apollo' camellias, 'Little Witch' daffodils, red and yellow 'Husky Mixed' primroses and Lonicera nitida 'Lemon Beauty'.*

YOU WILL NEED

Materials and tools
- Large galvanized tin bath, about 23cm (9in) high x 45cm (18in) wide x 60cm (24in) long
- Drill with bit for drilling metal
- Chunks of broken polystyrene
- Ericaceous potting compost
- String and short sticks (or canes)

Plants
- 2 x 'Apollo' camellias
- 3 x pots of 'Little Witch' daffodils
- 5 x pots of red and yellow 'Husky Mixed' primroses
- 1 x large (or 2 small) *Lonicera nitida* 'Lemon Beauty'

4 *Fill in with more ericaceous compost around the camellias' rootballs, then add the honeysuckle (Lonicera) at the front, angling its rootball so that its variegated foliage falls over the edge of the tin bath.*

5 *Using a stick to push back the honeysuckle foliage, clear a space to plant the daffodils and primroses. Plant the daffodils first. It doesn't matter if you lose a little compost around the bulbs.*

Charlie says…

Ericaceous plants like camellias enjoy seaweed-based feeds. So to keep them flowering, apply liquid feed every two or three weeks during the growing season. Never feed dry soil. Water first, then feed.

3 *Spread a 5cm (2in) layer of broken polystyrene chunks in the base, then add a layer of ericaceous compost. Place the camellias at the back, then tie up any floppy stems with string and short sticks.*

6 *Add compost to within 7.5cm (3in) of the rim, then fill in with a carpet of primroses. Again, tilt the plants forward a little so that the primroses hang over the rim of the tin bath. Firm in and water well.*

Ericaceous plants in pots

The word 'ericaceous' describes a group of lime-hating plants that includes camellias, summer heathers, rhododendrons, pieris and Japanese maples. If your soil is alkaline, which means it contains lime, or is sticky clay that lies wet in winter and dries rock hard in summer, you may have given up trying to grow lime-haters. But in containers you can create the perfect home for them. By providing the right compost you will keep their roots happy and by moving the pot around the garden you can give them just the right amount of sun, shade and shelter. The leaves of Japanese maples can be damaged by late spring frosts but if you grow your maple in a pot, you can move it to a sheltered corner when frost is forecast.

LIKE CAMELLIAS, JAPANESE MAPLES PREFER LIME-FREE SOIL

Camellias and companions

Pictured below are the plants I chose to fill my old tin bath. Planted together they make a bright and fresh spring display that will look good for six to eight weeks – the length of time the camellias will be in bloom. When choosing plants to team with your camellias balance their sizes. Select daffodils with flowers that will fill the gap around the bare stems of the camellias rather than tall varieties that will compete with the camellia for attention.

Keeping camellias happy in tubs
Camellias in tubs need a bit of tender loving care. The price for having these pretty plants in flower where you want them, is a little but regular attention to watering, feeding and position throughout the year. Just half a day's sun in the summer will encourage flower buds for the following year. Make sure you don't leave your plants in an east-facing site though. East-facing sites get strong early morning sun, and buds and blooms that are frosted

overnight and thaw out rapidly will discolour or shed. If your camellia flowers poorly in spring, it could be due to a lack of moisture – plants that got too dry in the summer may shed flower buds the next winter. Yellowing leaves can be caused by a lack of iron or magnesium. To remedy this, apply a liquid feed of sequestered iron.

AFTERCARE

Don't allow the compost in the tin bath display to dry out. If your tap water is hard, water with rain water or your camellias may suffer. (See page 29 for feeding tip.)

After flowering, transfer each camellia to a pot 5cm (2in) wider than its rootball, ready to use again the following year. If you want to save the primroses and daffodils, plant them out in a border. Split the daffodils up when planting – they will multiply and get better each year. Leave the lonicera in the tin bath as the basis for a summer display.

Honeysuckle
(*Lonicera nitida* 'Lemon Beauty')
You may be surprised to learn that this twiggy evergreen is a honeysuckle, because it bears little resemblance to the more familiar perfumed climber. It is low and spreading, which makes it ideal for groundcover in this display.

Daffodil
(*Narcissus* 'Little Witch')
This daffodil has the long trumpet and swept-back petals which are typical of the wild species *Narcissus cyclamineus*. Sturdy and upright, this plant is ideal for containers. Pot up bulbs in the autumn and plant them in your display in the spring.

Camellia
(*Camellia japonica* 'Apollo')
The flowers of this evergreen shrub appear in spring and have a profusion of overlapping petals that gives them an informal appearance. Plant camellias with the top of the rootball level with the compost – they don't like being buried too deep.

Florists' primroses
(*Primula vulgaris* 'Husky Mixed')
These large-flowered primroses are usually available through winter and spring and come in a range of colours. Each flower may have two or even three separate colours in its petals – perfect for a cheerful colour scheme.

Twining ivy topiary

Create a small living sculpture by growing ivy over a simple wire frame. With its bright new shoots in spring, ivy forms a lush green backdrop for fresh spring flowers.

Traditional topiary is usually on a grand scale – amazing shapes cut into large hedges in country-house gardens. But you can achieve a similar effect on a small scale by growing twining ivy around hand-made or ready-made wire frames and clipping it into shape.

The real beauty of ivy topiary is the speed with which it will cover a frame and grow into a plump little green sculpture. I think plants grown this way look attractive even before they have thickened up and taken on their final shape, which usually takes about 18 months. In contrast, the box shrubs commonly used for traditional topiary can take three years to grow from a cutting to a height of only 60cm (2ft).

WHEN TO PLANT – spring, after the last frosts

Making a topiary frame

When I first tackled ivy topiary, I started out with a simple hoop like the one shown in the steps. It's easier to bend wire into a circle than to make solid shapes, and the ivy will cover the circle faster.

When you are selecting an ivy for your topiary, choose one with several good, strong shoots. That way your topiary will have a head start and will certainly have at least a couple of shoots to wrap up each side of the hoop.

To get your ivy to grow thicker as it develops, pinch out the growing tips occasionally which encourages side shoots. To make sure your topiary grows evenly, turn your container regularly – to give all sides equal share of the sunlight.

Not all ivies are fully hardy, but if you have a light container, you can bring your topiary inside in winter if necessary.

More shapes

Once you've mastered a simple frame, if you're like me you'll probably want to try other shapes. Frames for spheres, cones and spirals are quite easy to make from strong wire or you can buy them ready-made from garden centres or florists. When I make the frames of solid shapes, such as cones or spheres, I use bent chicken wire and fill it with damp sphagnum moss. The ivy then clings to the moss and roots into it, making a strong, dense plant.

The aim of topiary is to cover the frame with ivy but to keep to the basic shape at the same time. So keep winding wayward shoots into the frame or you'll just end up with a blob of messy foliage. Once you've mastered the technique you can try something more adventurous, like a chicken or rabbit!

YOU WILL NEED

Materials and tools
- 25.5cm (10in) terracotta pot – plain or painted
- 2.5m (8ft) of firm, medium-weight plastic-coated or galvanized wire
- Wire cutters
- Pliers (optional)
- Broken crocks
- Multipurpose potting compost

Plants
- Ornamental ivy

1 To make the hoop frame, first straighten out any kinks in the wire so that you have a nice smooth length. Then shape the wire into a circle about 41cm (16in) in diameter, with two long loose ends of equal length.

2 Pinch the circle together where the two wires cross. Keeping the circle firmly pinched together, measure about 51cm (20in) from the point where the wires cross to each end and trim off the excess wire using the wire cutters.

3 At the base of the circle, begin twisting the wire ends around each other. Keep twisting until you have formed a stem at least 5cm (2in) long. If you find it too difficult to twist the wire by hand, use pliers to grip it.

Designing ivy topiary

A well-shaped topiary looks good on its own but often groups of three or more will give more impact. If you want to grow a whole set of ivy topiaries, first decide whether you want 'miniature' or larger shapes. Then choose containers to balance with the size of your frames. Topiary is a living garden sculpture and, as the container will be part of the creation, pick it with care to flatter your frame and ivy leaf shape. Some ready-made wire or willow topiary frames are so handsome on their own that they will look great even when only half covered with ivy. Bird-shaped frames look especially attractive when just planted up. Think of the leaf colouring too when growing a set of topiaries – I mix both solid-coloured and variegated leaves to add interest and energy to the grouping.

Display your topiary containers to fit in with the rest of your garden – in straight lines like soldiers for a smart tailored look or in relaxed arrangements to create a more casual atmosphere.

YOU CAN FORM EVEN QUITE MATURE IVIES INTO AN INTERESTING SHAPE – BUT PREFERABLY NOT WHEN IT'S RAINING!

4 *Bend the wire ends at right angles to the twisted stem, then bend them again to fit down into the pot. The stem should sit just proud of the top of the pot. Trim the ends again if necessary, and remove the wire frame.*

5 *Place a few broken crocks over the drainage hole, before filling the pot with compost. Plant the ivy in the centre so that it sits about 2.5cm (1in) below the top of the pot, and spread out the shoots. Push the frame legs into the compost.*

6 *Take the longest ivy shoot and gently twist it around the hoop starting at the frame stem. Repeat this process with the remaining shoots, twisting an equal number of shoots up each side of the hoop. Tuck in any loose ends. Water well.*

Types of ivy

For topiary, I prefer the small-leaved cultivars of English ivy (*Hedera helix*); these are usually quite hardy and easily available in a huge variety of leaf colours and forms. Ivies with variegated leaves need a reasonable amount of sunlight to keep their bright colours, and a sheltered spot in winter if possible. Most garden centres have a display of cheap young plants in pots with varying patterns of green and gold, silver or white. Look closely to see the variations, like edgings or marblings, and pick a selection of the same colour, or a mixture if you prefer. Ivies you buy at garden centres and florists aren't usually named, so what you see is what you get.

If you want something more up-market, you'll probably need to go to a specialist nursery where the ivy plants will be individually labelled. This is really worthwhile for finding some of the more unusual leaf shapes. Many of these less common varieties have all green leaves, so are especially good if your topiary is going to stand in shade. Grown in a border as groundcover, the interesting shapes of ivy leaves are not usually appreciated, but in a topiary pot they can be seen at close quarters and give an added interest to the structure. Some are frilly-edged, some sharply pointed like birds' feet and others have prominent veins. Check the hardiness of more unusual varieties as some will need extra protection in winter.

AFTERCARE

Don't let your ivy topiary dry out completely. Water frequently in the summer, especially if it's in full sun.

For strong, thick growth, feed your ivy with liquid foliar feed every month from late spring to early autumn.

It will take some months for the topiary to fill out into a plump shape, so it will not need trimming at first. Just twist the growing shoots in around the frame if they need encouragement. Trim ends only when the ivy starts to exceed the required shape.

VARIEGATED IVY LEAVES WILL SOFTEN THE EFFECT OF A FORMAL GEOMETRIC TOPIARY

BE CAREFUL HOW YOU TRIM YOUR IVY TOPIARY. TAKE CARE NOT TO CUT THROUGH INDIVIDUAL LEAVES AND SPOIL THEM

Classic style

Colourful perennials make a striking spring display – especially when planted in a large stylish stone urn and given pride of place on a pedestal.

When it comes to planting spring containers, most gardeners choose traditional favourites – bulbs such as daffodils, tulips and crocus, and bedding plants like primroses, pansies and double daisies. There's nothing wrong with that – they will make bright, cheerful displays. But for a look that's a little different, I like to plant up a selection of spring-flowering perennials in a stylish stone urn. Yellow leopard's bane and cowslips, indigo double primroses, dicentra and euphorbia will all come up year after year, so you can enjoy them in the urn in their first year and then, when they have finished flowering, plant them out perma-nently in the garden – great style and excellent value for money!

WHEN TO PLANT – early to mid spring

Planting the spring urn

In the spring, most garden centres will stock a range of perennials. You can buy them in bud, just showing flower colour, or in full bloom if you want an instant effect. For impact pack spring plants tightly into the urn with their rootballs touching each other. That way you get a really attractive, mature look right away. You can pack plants closely together for spring, autumn and winter displays, but summer displays need a little more space between the plants so they can spread adequately and get sufficient water.

Healthy plants

When buying perennials, whether for containers or the garden, always look for strong, healthy plants with bright green leaves. If you have time and patience, choose small plants –

usually sold in 9cm (3½ in) pots with just a few shoots. They are cheap, which is important if you need lots of plants, but will need to be potted up and grown on for a year before they are big enough to use in containers.

If you buy larger plants you can cut out the waiting and if you choose carefully you can often find a pot full of shoots that can be split into two or even three pieces. Popular perennials like hostas are often available as extra large plants – ideal for containers.

Next year's spring urn

If you don't need your urn for a summer display, leave the plants there for next year. Most perennials will be perfectly happy in the same container for 2-3 years, as long as they have room to spread. If they get a little crowded just remove one or two.

YOU WILL NEED

Materials and tools
- Urn 45cm (18in) in diameter and at least 15cm (6in) deep
- Pedestal (optional)
- Multipurpose potting compost

Plants
- 2 x spurge (*Euphorbia* x *martinii*)
- 1 x Dutchman's breeches (*Dicentra spectabilis*)
- 2 x leopard's bane (*Doronicum* 'Little Leo')
- 2 x double primrose (*Primula* 'Miss Indigo')
- 4 x cowslip (*Primula veris*)

To invigorate established perennials in a container, scrape away the top 5cm (2in) of old compost in spring and replace it with fresh potting compost. After the second or third year, in early summer when the

1 *If you are planning to put your display on a pedestal, position it in sun or semi-shade and put the urn on top. Then fill the urn with compost to within about 5cm (2in) of the rim.*

2 *Select your plants, choosing healthy specimens like these, preferably just coming into bloom but with plenty of buds to come. A mixture of shapes and colours will give a fresh-looking display.*

3 *Start by planting the two euphorbias as far back in the urn as they will go. When handling these plants, wear gloves, because the milky sap that oozes from damaged tissue is an irritant.*

Spring perennial displays

flowers have finished, take the plants out and transfer them to permanent positions in your garden. The plants will come up again year after year and, if you like, you can even put them back in a new container display a few years on.

Charlie says...

Many stone urns are rather shallow, so mound the compost up a little in the centre. But don't bury the rootballs any deeper than they were in their original pots.

Regular deadheading will keep your display looking good for longer, but avoid cutting off sideshoots growing below faded flowers – they will produce a second flush of bloom.

4 *Plant the dicentra in the centre between the two euphorbias, then tuck in the two doronicums. Add the primulas, filling in with more compost as you go. Water in well.*

I love to experiment with different combinations of spring perennials. Double primroses *Primula vulgaris* and *Primula* 'Easter Bonnet' look wonderful with the celandine *Ranunculus ficaria* 'Randall's White', thrift (*Armeria maritima*), and, for interesting foliage, heuchera and lords and ladies (*Arum italicum*). In the containers for this *Ground Force* garden I planted spring-flowering broom with pansies and primulas. The brilliant spring colours looked great in modern galvanized containers.

THIS SPRING DISPLAY WAS AN INSTANT SUCCESS AND MADE GOOD USE OF SIMPLE BUT STYLISH SQUARE-TOPPED CONTAINERS

Perennials for our classic urn

Planting containers with a variety of perennials is a really good way to familiarize yourself with a wide range of plants of different heights, habits and colours. To create a lively show, full of interest, you need an element of contrast in your display. For spring colour, the plants I have selected for the urn are among the best. They all grow best in sun or semi-shade, and include the four plants shown here plus leopard's bane (*Doronicum*), the first daisy of the spring.

You will be surprised at how long these herbaceous plants keep on flowering. Dutchman's breeches will entertain you with its elegant, arching stems hung with flowers like pendant lockets for at least a month. Leopard's bane produces a succession of daisy blooms for two months, while the spurge outlasts them all and still looks good in mid summer.

When planting double primroses, angle the rosettes of leaves towards you so they soften the pot rim and show the flowers full on.

AFTERCARE

Keep the compost moist. A container in full sun and exposed to wind will dry out more quickly than one in shelter and shade.

Snip off the flowers on the doronicums and primroses as they fade. Pull off any yellowing primrose leaves, as they can cause rot to spread into the crown.

To collect seed from the cowslips when it is ripe, shake it from the seedheads into an envelope. Sow the seed straight away in a seed tray.

After flowering, you can carefully lift all the plants out of your urn and plant them in your garden. Choose a semi-shaded spot and enrich the soil with a good covering of old potting compost or well-rotted garden compost before planting.

Spurge
(*Euphorbia x martinii*)
This is a superb, upright plant with yellow-green bracts surrounding the tiny dark red flowers. It reaches its full height of 90cm (3ft) in its second year. Handle with gloves and wear goggles when pruning.

Double primrose
(*Primula* 'Miss Indigo')
One of the best of the double primroses, 'Miss Indigo' has the advantage of remaining tight and compact – unlike some varieties whose flowers and leaves stretch out and become untidy.

Dutchman's breeches
(*Dicentra spectabilis*)
The shape of these flowers has resulted in many common names, including Dutchman's breeches and bleeding heart. Take care when handling this plant as the stems are brittle and can easily snap. There is also a white form.

Cowslip
(*Primula veris*)
Cowslips are a classic and prolific spring flower, even seeding in lawns if left to their own devices. The height and colour of the flowers are variable from seed, so if you like these copper and orange tints, wait until plants show colour before buying.

Herb tower

Herbs smell wonderful in the garden and many are a distinct bonus for the chef as well. Growing them in this stylish tower will make them easier to tend and pick.

When we're working on *Ground Force* gardens we're often asked to plant herbs, but they can be invasive. The beauty of your own container-grown herbs is that as well as cutting out the cost of buying fresh herbs from the supermarket, you will also have herbs 'on tap' whenever you need them and they won't take over the garden.

This space-saving tower with its tiered design is made from three separate pots stacked on top of each other. With this design you can fit a lot of different plants into a small area, and it's easy to maintain. An attractive planter brimming with edible and fragrant leaves, kept in a sunny spot near the kitchen door, is sure to please both the chef and the gardener.

WHEN TO PLANT – **spring, after the last frosts**

Making the herb tower

Before buying the three pots for your tower, check the sizes very carefully. The top two each need to be small enough to fit inside the one below without looking skimpy. The square-topped containers I found make a particularly impressive tower, but round ones will work equally well. The finished tower is quite heavy, so plant it up in its final position.

Most herbs originate from hot, Mediterranean countries and grow best in full sun, so choose a sunny position for your planter, as close to the kitchen as possible.

1 *Put a 5-8cm (2-3in) layer of gravel in each pot to help with drainage. Then push a cane through the gravel into the hole in the base of the largest pot, and fill with compost to within 2.5cm (1in) of the top.*

2 *Line up the drainage hole of the middle pot with the cane and slide it down the cane until it rests on the soil in the bottom pot. Fill the middle pot with compost to within 2.5cm (1in) of the top.*

3 *Plant the top pot. This will be the focal point, so look for plants with shape and impact – for example, sage, chervil, rocket, chives or dill. For extra colour, you could try purple sage or basil.*

4 *Cut the cane with a junior hacksaw so it is just long enough to hold the top pot in position. Disturbing the roots as little as possible, place the top pot over the cane to rest on the soil below.*

5 *For the middle pot, choose herbs that aren't too tall, such as feverfew, thyme and parsley. Plant them close together for an instant effect, or space out young plants so they have room to grow.*

6 *Plant up the bottom pot with your chosen herbs. Then water each pot well. In time, to help fill gaps left between perennial herbs after harvesting, drop in annual herbs, such as rocket and basil.*

Edible flowers

Charlie says…

During the summer, container-grown herbs will benefit from a liquid seaweed-based feed every two weeks or so. If you want a continual supply of leaves, try not to let your herbs flower. Pick off flower buds as they form to keep your herbs producing healthy leaves for as long as possible.

If you like the idea of a continuous supply of fresh herbs but still want some colourful flowers, why not plant up your tower with a mixture of herbs and decorative, edible flowering plants?

Pot marigolds (*Calendula officinalis*) are delicious in salads and you can use the flowers instead of saffron to give rice a lovely, golden yellow colour. Nasturtiums (*Tropaeolum majus*) are another favourite of mine – the flowers, seeds and spicy leaves look and taste great in a salad. Sweet violet flowers (*Viola odorata*) can be candied, made into jellies and jams or used to flavour sugar or vinegar. The fragrant spikes of lavender can look striking in the top pot and the flowers can be used sparingly to flavour sugar or vinegar, too. Succulent alpine strawberries tumbling over the sides will also look and taste wonderful.

Just one word of warning when selecting plants – always check carefully that you have chosen a variety that is completely safe to eat.

DON'T STICK TO HERBS ALONE. ADD SOME FLOWERS IN YOUR TOWER FOR COLOUR, SCENT AND TASTE

Herb selection

To fill a terracotta herb tower the same size as mine, you'll need at least eight different types of herb plants. Base your choice of herbs around those you use most often in the kitchen, starting with the four useful ones shown below and some parsley. Remember that perennial herbs may last for several years, but annuals will die down and need to be replaced each spring. Keep an open mind – a plant may catch your eye because of an unusual leaf colour or form that will add interest to the display. Be sure to buy enough plants to fill all three tiers, and when you get the herbs home, give them a good water before you replant them in the tower.

AFTERCARE

Although herbs hate sitting in waterlogged soil, all containers need watering well, especially in hot, dry or windy weather. The best time to water is early morning.

Prune regularly and snip off flowerheads to keep your herbs compact and encourage new, well-flavoured growth.

Triple pots of style

One of the reasons we use pebbles and shingles in the *Ground Force* gardens is because their natural, soft tones make such a good contrast against pots and plants. Try this eye-catching idea. Plant up three different herbs, or one herb, one conifer and one periwinkle, group the pots together, set them at angles and you have an instant feature.

Common thyme
(*Thymus vulgaris* 'Silver Posie')
Low-growing. Other varieties, such as lemon thyme, are also worth trying. Usually evergreen, so can be picked any time of year. In summer, if you leave the purple flowers on they will attract butterflies.

Rosemary
(*Rosmarinus officinalis*)
Will grow into a shrub fairly quickly but regular harvesting and pruning will help curtail its size. Likes full sun. New growth will appear early each year. Small, blue flowers in summer. Very strongly flavoured.

Sage
(*Salvia officinalis* 'Tricolor', *S.o.* 'Purpurascens', *S.o.* 'Aurea')
Another sun-lover, sage is an evergreen plant which can get a bit woody over time. Has lots of aromatic foliage. Tricolor sage, golden sage and purple sage – shown above – are all worth growing.

Golden oregano
(*Origanum vulgare* 'Aureum')
One of several oregano varieties. Oregano and sweet marjoram are closely related – the latter (*Origanum majorana*) has a milder, sweeter flavour. Both grow year after year and thrive in a hot, sunny position.

Traditional planter

For late spring make a 'hot-coloured' display of tulips, pansies and wallflowers. The planting is done in stages starting in late summer the previous year.

One of the best ways to create an eye-catching spring container that will really stand out in your garden is to pack a large pot with a fiery collection of red and yellow flowers. For maximum impact, position your display against a plain background – it's ideal for drawing attention away from a wall or brightening up an evergreen hedge.

The star attractions of this arrangement are the bright-coloured tulips – Rembrandt Mix, which has vivid yellow petals licked with red, flame-like markings, and red 'Carlton', an early double variety. The parrot tulip 'Texas Flame' is even more flamboyant and would make a good alternative to either of these.

As companions for the tulips, I added *Euphorbia griffithii* 'Fireglow' and some tall wallflowers in shades of red, yellow and orange. Yellow, black-centred pansies were perfect for filling the base of the display.

WHEN TO PLANT – in stages from late summer to mid spring

Creating the display

This display needs to be planned well ahead, as the tulip bulbs and wallflowers are planted the year before, but the extra effort is well worth it. Wallflower plants are available from late summer in garden centres, either growing in pots or as bundles of bare-rooted plants. If you get bare-rooted plants, soak the roots in water for about an hour before you pot up the plants three to a 15cm (2 litre) pot.

Plant the tulip bulbs in late autumn, three or four bulbs to a 15cm (2 litre) plastic pot. It isn't necessary to use fresh compost – I often use old compost from tomato growing bags for this stage. Just before you're ready to plant the display in mid spring, buy the euphorbia and pots of pansies already in bloom.

Bulbs for spring colour

Buying a large ornamental container is a big outlay so make sure you like the design enough to use it for displays throughout the year, not just for one with a single season life span like this arrangement. One clever idea is a 'never-ending' spring bulb display. By combining early-, middle- and late-flowering bulbs you can have the ultimate low-maintenance container. The bulbs can all be planted at the same time in the autumn, directly into the container, left throughout the winter, to appear in spring needing no more than an occasional watering.

Choose crocus for early spring, joined by dwarf daffodils such as *Narcissus* 'Jack Snipe' or 'Topolino', and mid to late season tulips like 'Apricot Beauty' or 'Blue Heron'. This combination will flower from very early spring to early summer. Add spring-flowering violas, pansies or primroses as companion plants and enjoy.

YOU WILL NEED

Materials
- 15cm (2 litre) pots for pre-planting
- Large decorative pot, 45cm (18in) in diameter and at least 30cm (12in) deep
- Chunks of broken polystyrene
- Multipurpose potting compost

Plants
- 3 x pots of tall mixed wallflowers
- 10 x *Tulipa* Rembrandt Mix bulbs or other tall red and yellow tulip
- 10 x *Tulipa* 'Carlton' bulbs
- 1 x *Euphorbia griffithii* 'Fireglow'
- 5 x pots of yellow and black pansies

1 Start preparing the display the year before. Buy and plant the wallflowers (as explained above) in late summer and plant the tulip bulbs in the late autumn, so they're ready for the following spring.

2 In early to mid spring, move a large frost-proof container to a sunny, sheltered spot. Either roll it on the ground like this or pull it along on a sack. Buy pansies and euphorbia ready for planting.

3 Put a layer of polystyrene chunks in the bottom for drainage and cover with compost. Then knock all the plants out of their plastic pots, plant them carefully in the container and water in well.

Charlie says...

Unlike daffodil bulbs, which dry out if stored, tulip bulbs fare better if taken out of the ground after flowering. You can then store them to plant out again in very late autumn. This makes the bulbs less likely to suffer from tulip fire disease. Diseased bulbs should be destroyed.

AFTERCARE

To keep the tulips for another year, plant them in the garden when the petals have fallen and they are past their best. When they have completely died down, lift and store the bulbs.

After the wallflowers and tulips have flowered, replace the wallflowers with sweet williams. You can leave the pansies and euphorbia in the pot for another six weeks or so.

4 For the sake of neatness and to reduce the risk of tulip fire disease, remove the tulip petals as they are about to fall or when they have just fallen. When the display is over follow the Aftercare tips.

Tulips in buckets

I find lots of unusual and attractive containers in junk shops. They are usually very cheap to buy and look great filled with spring bulbs. It doesn't matter if they are slightly damaged with cracks and dents, as long as they have a good flat base so they will stand firmly upright. In a bucket like this I usually make about eight to ten holes for drainage, using a large nail and a hammer.

This bucket display features red *Tulipa* 'Red Riding Hood', they are one of my favourites – extremely reliable with vibrant flowers. For contrast I planted a silvery leaved ornamental nettle, *Lamium* 'Hermann's Pride', in the centre.

This ornamental nettle is evergreen, so it provides a carpet of colour all winter and then starts attractive new growth just when the tulips are in bloom. You can plant the bulbs and nettle directly into the container in the late autumn and it will look its best in mid spring. When planting the bulbs either follow the instructions on the pack or plant them twice their depth in the ground. Arrange them in a circle so they are close but not touching.

Turn up the heat

Here are profiles of four of the hot-coloured plants I chose for the large decorative container. I also included some tall spring-flowering mixed wallflowers (*Erysimum*). These for me capture the essence of a cottage garden in spring. They have a delicious, intense perfume and come in a range of ravishing colours.

Keep the heat on

If you like the idea of setting off more fireworks in your spring containers, there are plenty of other really hot customers around. Bulbs, especially tulips, are prime candidates. In smaller containers the exotic red and white dwarf tulip 'Johann Strauss' makes a good hot centrepiece when surrounded with small purple and yellow violas. For hanging baskets and window boxes, try some of the delightful miniatures like the yellow and white *Tulipa tarda*, the riotous red *Tulipa linifolia* and the soft yellow, cinnamon-shaded *Tulipa linifolia* Batalinii Group 'Bright Gem'.

An easy way to make tulips the centrepiece of a slightly more subtle spring display is to base your scheme on the single colour of a classy variety like the lovely rich pink *Tulipa* 'Kees Nelis'. Pop the bulbs into individual pots in the autumn, then plant them out along the back of a blue trough in late March. Choose some pink Accolade buttercups from the garden centre for a row in front of the tulips. Then edge the front of the trough with pink double daisies.

Pansy Universal Series
(*Viola* Universal Series)
From the Universal strain, this pansy is outstanding in its ability to flower in the autumn, intermittently in the winter, then freely in spring. Pick off the faded flowers before they turn into green seedpods to encourage continued flowering. After the spring flush of blooms the pansies will become leggy and are best discarded.

Spurge
(*Euphorbia griffithii* 'Fireglow')
A real head turner in May and June, this plant can be grown for several years in a pot. Expect a height of 60cm (24in). Be careful to avoid contact with the milky sap as it can irritate the skin and eyes.

Tulip Rembrandt Mix
A tall variety reaching up to 60cm (24in) high, these tulips are noted for their attractive streaked and feathered petals. These are the sort of bulbs that changed hands for vast sums at the height of their popularity in Holland centuries ago.

Tulip 'Carlton'
Sturdy and compact at around 30cm (12in) tall, 'Carlton' is a favourite for its showy nature and long-lasting blooms. It is great value for money and can be bought on its own or often as part of a mixed pack of tulip bulbs.

Picket window box

This picket window box is actually a surround that's perfect for concealing an inexpensive plastic trough. It looks great painted to match the colour scheme of your planting.

Finding just the right container for your windowsill isn't always easy. All too often, they're the wrong size or colour or the one you like is prohibitively expensive. This simple, miniature picket fence seems to me to be the perfect solution. It is custom built to fit your windowsill, can be painted to suit the colour of your house, or your planting, and will disguise the container behind it.

The spring colour scheme here is centred on the jaunty yellow narcissus and polyanthus which are sparked off against blue hyacinths and dark green ivy. Although you can grow the narcissus and hyacinths from bulbs started in pots the previous autumn, it's much easier to buy them, and the polyanthus, as plants in early spring. They're all hardy, so frost won't hurt them. As the flowers won't look their best for very long, for displays like this I often leave the plants in their individual pots and just sink them in compost. I used plenty of plants for a bold effect, with trailing ivies to soften the edges.

WHEN TO PLANT – **early spring**

Making the picket surround

You may not fancy yourself as a carpenter, but have a go at making this fabulous picket fence. It needs to fit your sill exactly, so before beginning the steps, measure the width and depth of your sill carefully – always measure the width of the sill at the back nearest to the window. Make a full-size paper template of the sill, using newspaper or, for long sills, an off-cut of wallpaper.

For a two-colour picket surround, you will need an odd number of pickets for the front, so start by calculating the number of 50mm wide picket slats you need, allowing about 20mm between them. Larger gaps between the pickets will defeat the purpose, which is to hide the trough.

Next, calculate the number of pickets needed for the sides, again allowing about 20mm between pickets. The two front batten supports that the pickets are nailed to should be 70mm shorter than the width of

the sill, and the four side battens (two at each end) should be 35mm shorter than the depth of the sill – this allows for the width of the corner battens and side pickets.

The quantities of wood given in the list on the right are for a sill 1030mm wide and 200mm deep, so be sure to buy more if your windowsill is bigger.

Choosing a container

A tough plastic trough that is as big as possible and will still fit behind the picket surround is best. Dark-coloured containers are less visible through the picket gaps than light ones, and green blends well with foliage.

YOU WILL NEED

Materials and tools
- Prepared softwood for a sill 200mm x 1030mm: 6.8m of 9mm x 50mm (pickets); 3m of 9mm x 32mm (batten supports); 600mm of 25 x 25mm (corner battens)
- 16mm and 32mm panel pins
- 38mm No 8 screws
- Exterior wood-preservative stain, in lavender and yellow
- Metal ruler and pencil
- G-clamp and workbench or table
- Hammer and screwdriver
- Hand saw and sandpaper
- Paintbrush
- Drill with wood and masonry bits
- Wall plugs

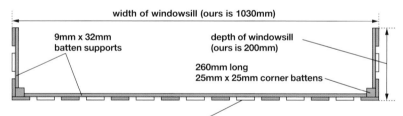

width of windowsill (ours is 1030mm)

9mm x 32mm batten supports

depth of windowsill (ours is 200mm)

260mm long 25mm x 25mm corner battens

300mm long x 9mm x 50mm picket slats

Charlie says…

It's easy to change your display with the seasons – just lift out one trough and pop in the next or simply replant. For summer colour try busy lizzies, trailing geraniums and ivy (see right). For a winter display, leave the ivies in the trough, but replace the summer flowers with topiaried rosemary and cyclamens (see far right).

1 Calculate the number of pickets you need. Then cut a 300mm long slat for each picket from 9mm by 50mm softwood. Then draw a 35mm deep point at one end of one slat.

2 Use a G-clamp to secure the marked picket slat to your workbench or table – this will keep it steady and make accurate cutting easier. Then cut the shaped point along the pencil lines using a hand saw.

3 Sand the edges of the shaped point of this first picket, which will be used as a template. You can wrap the sandpaper around a block of wood to keep the sanded edges straight and flat.

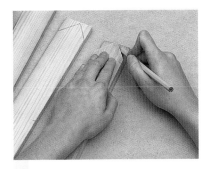

4 Use the 'template' to mark a point on all the pickets. Cut as before. Next cut two front and four side batten supports from 9mm by 32mm softwood, and two corner battens 260mm long from 25mm by 25mm wood. Sand all cut edges.

5 Decide how many lavender and how many yellow pickets you need. Paint the yellow pickets with two coats. Then paint the remaining pickets and all the batten pieces with two coats of lavender. Leave the paint to dry thoroughly.

6 Lay the two front battens 100mm apart and position the pickets. The end pickets need to extend 34mm past the batten ends to allow for the 25mm corner batten and one 9mm thick picket. Nail on the pickets with 16mm panel pins.

7 Nail the side pickets to their battens in the same way, this time allowing for a 25mm slot for the corner batten (see diagram). With 32mm panel pins, nail the two corner battens to the back of the end pickets of the front, 9mm from the edge.

8 Slot the sides of the picket surround on to the front so that the end pickets touch at the corners as shown in the diagram. Carefully, nail the end side pickets to the square corner battens using 32mm panel pins.

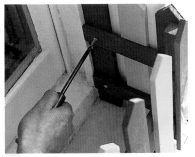

9 To fit the surround to the sill, first drill one pilot hole through each of the two side battens and mark the wall through these holes. Drill into the wall at the marked points and insert wall plugs. Then fix the surround with 38mm No 8 screws.

Summer

Summer colour

When summer arrives and the danger of frost is over, I can't wait to set out all the pots of plants I've been growing or the ones I found too hard to resist when buying for a *Ground Force* programme. With so many plants to choose from, decide what you want from your summer containers and how much effort you are prepared to put in to achieve it before you buy that expensive but impractical plant.

Bedding plants like busy lizzies and petunias can be raised from seed, or bought as plugs or as pot-ready bedding. If you're a keen gardener, with patience and a heated propagator, you can grow plants from seed. It may be time-consuming, but you will be able to find more unusual varieties from seed catalogues than on sale as plants in a garden centre. Plug plants are inexpensive and a great idea. They are small seedlings that come ready to pot up, so they are ideal if you only want a few (unlike with seeds where you often end up throwing unwanted seedlings away). Pot-ready plants are the most expensive but quickest way to plant up summer containers, and the only option for us when preparing containers for a *Ground Force* garden.

Summer containers can be colourful with massed flowering plants like busy lizzies; exotic, filled with palms, cannas and castor oil plants; traditional, blending fragrant lavender, lilies, scented-leaved pelargoniums and pinks; or cool and contemplative with Japanese maples, hostas and *Fatsia japonica* in oriental glazed pots.

When choosing plants, be practical about what will grow where. Most flowering plants prefer full sun, so if your container is destined to brighten a shady corner, go for fuchsias, begonias and astilbes for flowers and hostas and ferns for their luxuriant foliage.

If you want hanging baskets but are likely to be away for long weekends, think again. Hanging baskets are high maintenance, so if you're not around to give them a daily watering, substitute fleshy-leaved succulents for petunias and lobelia, or set up an automatic irrigation system.

MUST-HAVE PLANTS FOR SUMMER CONTAINERS

Agave americana 'Marginata'	*Lilium* 'Star Gazer'
Brachyscome multifida	New Guinea busy lizzies
Canna 'Striata'	Parsley
Cordyline australis 'Torbay Dazzler'	*Pelargonium* 'Frank Headley'
Fuchsia 'Thalia'	Petunia 'Purple Wave'
Hakonechloa macra 'Aureola'	*Rosa* Flower Carpet series
Hosta 'Wide Brim'	*Rosa* 'Irish Eyes'
Lavandula stoechas subsp. *pedunculata*	Rosemary
	Tomato 'Tumbler'
	Viola 'Orchid Frost'

Summer hanging basket

Create a colourful combination of pink busy lizzies and deep blue lobelia in your hanging basket. It's an eye-catching mixture with a big impact and a low budget.

Busy lizzies and lobelia are both easy-care plants that come in a wide range of colours. Take a trip around your local garden centre in the spring and early summer and you should be spoilt for choice. If you are anything like me you will buy far too many plants and end up giving away baskets to all your family and friends!

You don't have to buy a lot of plants to get a spectacular flower-packed basket. The plants may look small when you put them in, but within a few weeks of planting they will bush out and you'll have a basket that's the envy of your neighbours. With regular feeding and frequent watering, the flowers will keep going well into the autumn.

WHEN TO PLANT – any time after the last frosts in late spring

Hanging basket know-how

This hanging basket display is simple to plant, easy to care for, good to look at and, if you buy your plants in polystyrene bedding strips rather than pots, the cost is very reasonable. You get a lot of plants for your money in a bedding strip and, because the roots of plants grown in strips are still small, you'll find planting them through the sides of the basket is no problem. With small clumps of lobelia it is easy to feed the roots

1 *Press a thick layer of moss, coco fibre or sisal into the bottom of the basket and a third of the way up the sides. Put the small circle of plastic over the moss at the bottom of the basket. This will act as a water reservoir for the roots.*

2 *Add a couple of handfuls of potting compost mixed with water-retaining gel. Then put in the first ring of plants level with the liner. Use three clumps each of lobelia and busy lizzie alternately around the basket.*

3 *Add a collar of moss around each plant, tucking it in place around the base of the stem. Check the roots remain in contact with the compost. Continue the moss to two thirds up the sides of the basket. Add compost to the same level.*

4 *Add the next layer of plants – three of each type – and stagger the planting so that a lobelia sits above a busy lizzie and vice versa. Tuck moss around the plant stems as before, then extend the moss to about 2.5cm (1in) above the rim.*

5 *Finish by planting four clumps of each plant in the top of the basket. Add more compost, pressing down gently between each plant. Water well and firm down. Fill any gaps in the moss. Leave to drain thoroughly before hanging.*

YOU WILL NEED

Materials and tools
- Wire hanging basket, 35cm (14in) in diameter
- Moss, coco fibre or sisal liner
- Circle of plastic cut from an old compost bag or similar
- Multipurpose potting compost
- Water-retaining gel
- Small pieces of paper or plastic to protect leaves as you plant

Plants
- 10 x pink busy lizzies (*Impatiens* 'Accent Rose')
- 10 x deep blue, clump-forming, bush lobelia (*Lobelia* 'Crystal Palace')

through the gaps in the wire. If you have a problem with larger plants, try wrapping the leaves in a small tube of plastic or paper to protect them. Then you can push the tube out through the wires leaving the roots inside the basket.

This planting scheme will grow into a lovely ball-shaped basket. Site it so that it can be enjoyed at eye level and not just viewed from underneath. When you hang it up make sure it is secure – it will be very heavy when it is watered.

Charlie says…

This basket loves to be fed and watered regularly. It is almost impossible to overfeed busy lizzies, so from about four weeks after planting, give them a weekly liquid feed with a tomato fertilizer. The basket should be watered frequently; daily in very hot or windy weather. It is best to water in the evening or early morning if you can. Try not to water in direct sunlight or you may scorch the flowers and leaves. Using water-retaining gel in the compost will help keep the roots moist and happy.

A white theme

Using mainly white-flowered plants makes the budget basket below a very classy affair. For this planting I've used crisp white busy lizzies instead of the pink ones in the main display. I've used mainly white lobelia too – just dotting the occasional mauve lobelia plant in so they stand out like jewels. The variegated leaves of pineapple mint add further bright highlights. These plants are fabulous for both light and shady settings. There is a risk of the mint scorching in bright sunlight, but the delicious, fruity fragrance far outweighs any inconvenience. Again, all the plants are available in polystyrene strips which should keep the price right down.

WHITE TRAILING LOBELIA AND BUSY LIZZIES WITH FRAGRANT MINT

Take your pick of the plants

You really are spoilt for choice when it comes to lobelias and busy lizzies. The colour combinations are as exciting as they are endless.

Lobelia is available in white, purple, pale and deep blues, carmine-red, pink and mixed colours, such as 'String of Pearls Mixed', below right. Whether you are looking for a compact bushy plant or a trailing one for your basket, there's a variety of lobelia to fit the bill. Lobelias come from South Africa where they are perennial plants, but in the UK they are usually treated as half-hardy annuals and planted out once there is little risk of frost.

For busy lizzies, the list of colours goes on and on. They range from red through burgundy, cranberry, rose, pink, salmon, orange, apricot, white, violet, lavender and purple. Plus, there are all the fancy two-toned petal patterns. Busy lizzies are probably the most popular summer bedding plants in the world. They are certainly the most versatile. They do equally well in sun and shade and go on until cut down by autumn frosts.

Both plants will tolerate shade or full sun – though they prefer somewhere sheltered. What is more, they are remarkably undemanding and easy to care for.

AFTERCARE

Once planted, this basket should not be placed outdoors at night until all risk of frost has passed. The warmer and more sheltered the site, the better the basket will thrive.

Feed and water regularly (see page 55).

There is no need to deadhead busy lizzies as they will shed their petals, but you might like to remove all seedheads once or twice in high summer to encourage continued flowering.

Blue lobelia
(*Lobelia* 'Crystal Palace')
Lobelia 'Crystal Palace' has a mass of wonderful, deep blue flowers with bronze shading on the leaves. It is a neat, clump-forming lobelia. Planting this helps to create a good ball-shaped flowering hanging basket.

Mixed lobelia
(*Lobelia* 'String of Pearls Mixed')
This variety produces a kaleidoscope of colours, including crimson, lilac, white, and light and dark blue, which makes a stunning background for one of the more vibrant busy lizzies.

Pink busy lizzie
(*Impatiens* 'Accent Rose')
Accent Series busy lizzies are low growing which makes them perfect for hanging baskets. They also have an exceptionally long flowering season. This one has brilliant rose-pink flowers that deepen in colour towards the centre.

Two-toned busy lizzie
(*Impatiens* 'Pink Frost')
Edged in rich pink, these two-tone flowers have subtle pale pink centres. Even in a shady corner, 'Pink Frost' will produce abundant flowers right up to the first frosts of winter.

Setting the standard

A standard rose in an attractive container makes a display with a difference. It's ideal for creating a colourful focal point or for brightening up an otherwise dull corner.

Roses can really light up your garden and your life. For me, their blowsy, often perfumed, blooms capture the very essence of summer. Recently, the popularity of roses seems to have waned in favour of perennials like hostas and ornamental grasses, but for real summer flower power I don't think you can beat a rose.

If you haven't been rose shopping for some time, look out for the new generation of robust, free-flowering and disease-resistant varieties. The lovely yellow rose Flower Carpet 'Sunshine' used in this display is one such variety. You will often see it for sale in bush form and it makes dense groundcover. Buy it budded on to a tall stem to make a standard and its semi-weeping nature will be revealed in a pretty cascade.

Even a perfect rose will benefit from a few select companions around its roots. The ones playing supporting roles here are an upright hosta and smoke bush, plus trailing bellflowers and creeping Jenny.

WHEN TO PLANT – early summer

Creating your rose display

I think this beautiful display deserves a special container so I've selected a terracotta one that's decorated with a design of cherubs and swags. Make sure you choose a solid container too, as standard roses are top heavy and a plastic container may blow over in strong winds. If you do use a plastic pot, put some stones or bricks in the bottom when you add the drainage material and before you put in the compost. This should stop your display falling over.

Nurseries grow roses nowadays in deep pots, so take the hint and grow yours in a container that is at least 40cm (16in) deep – this will give the roots the space they need. If you keep your standard rose display for several years, you will have to move the rose to a bigger pot. It is best to do this in the autumn. A half barrel

with a 60cm (24in) diameter will provide the volume and depth of compost to keep the standard growing well. Once you have moved your rose to a bigger pot, tie it to a 2.5cm (1in) square stake for support.

1 Choose a pot big enough for the rootball of the standard rose and the other plants. For instant effect, buy a rose in bud, or even in flower.

YOU WILL NEED

Materials and tools
- Large terracotta container
- Chunks of broken polystyrene
- Multipurpose potting compost
- Piece of garden fleece

Plants
- 1 x standard rose (*Rosa* Flower Carpet 'Sunshine')
- 1 x hosta (*Hosta* 'Wide Brim')
- 1 x creeping Jenny (*Lysimachia nummularia* 'Aurea')
- 1 x bellflower (*Campanula poscharskyana*)
- 1 x smoke bush (*Cotinus coggygria* 'Golden Spirit')

4 Put the hosta in the gap between the pot edge and the rose rootball. You may need to loosen and pull away some of the compost from around its roots.

Rose companions

I chose the combination of plants under the rose to reflect the colour of the rose blooms. But do try some favourites of your own. The classic accompaniments to roses are

2 Tip the rose over and check beneath the branches for any yellow or brown dying shoots. Snip them off with secateurs to prevent the dieback from spreading.

5 Wrap the hosta in garden fleece to give yourself room to manoeuvre, then add the two trailing plants – the creeping Jenny and the bellflower– and the cotinus.

lavender and lady's mantle (*Alchemilla mollis*). Their blue and yellow tones seem to work with almost any colour of rose and the lavender gives the added bonus of a delicious scent.

3 *Put a 5cm (2in) layer of broken polystyrene in the base of your pot for drainage. Add a layer of compost, then place the rose and its cane on top.*

6 *Remove the garden fleece from around the hosta leaves. Spread the leaves out carefully and arrange the blue trails of campanula. Water well.*

Buying roses

You can buy your rose as a bare-rooted plant in autumn or winter. Most rose specialists sell plants this way, so you'll have a wider choice than if you buy container-grown plants. They are cheaper, too. But with container-grown roses (on sale from spring to summer) you do get to see and smell the flowers before buying. When buying roses, look for bushy plants with an even spread of shoots extending in all directions and healthy foliage. A good standard rose will have shoots growing from three points around the top of the stem.

MAKE SURE YOU CHOOSE A HEALTHY PLANT WHEN BUYING A CONTAINER-GROWN ROSE

Roses and partners

There are some beautiful roses that are ideal for growing in pots. These include the spreading groundcover types, dainty miniatures and larger flowered but compact patio varieties. All will be enhanced by suitable companions. Here are more details on the plants I've used in the rose display, plus an alternative pure white Flower Carpet rose which is another of my favourites.

To keep your rose in tip-top condition, watch out for greenfly attacks. These little pests appear on young rose buds and shoots very early in the year. You can control them with an insecticidal soap. And if your rose develops black spot, help prevent black spot fungal spores being carried over from one year to the next by gathering up all fallen rose leaves and putting them in the dustbin. Don't put them on your compost heap.

AFTERCARE

Water your standard rose display regularly, especially during hot, dry weather. A foliar feed applied through a sprayer will act as a quick pick-me-up for all the plants in the arrangement.

Deadheading the roses is not essential as the petals are shed naturally, but trimming back spent shoots by a third means new buds will develop. These will carry a new flush of blooms so it's worth taking time to do this.

Rosa Flower Carpet 'Sunshine'
The flower buds on this delicately perfumed rose will form continuously throughout the summer. It has good disease resistance. Expect a height and spread of around 90cm (3ft).

Smoke bush
(*Cotinus coggygria* 'Golden Spirit')
This upright bush with paddle-shaped leaves can reach 2.1m (7ft) in height and spread so you will have to move it out of your rose display after one season.

Rosa Flower Carpet white
This is the white representative in the Flower Carpet series. It has the same bushy habit and ability to flower through the summer and well into autumn – weather permitting. It grows to around 60cm (2ft) tall with a 90cm (3ft) spread.

Hosta 'Wide Brim'
This fine dwarf hosta has leaves with an irregular outline of cream and it is topped by lavender-blue flowers in summer. If well fed and watered, it will grow happily in a container for years.

Bellflower
(*Campanula poscharskyana*)
An easily grown, vigorous perennial, this trailing bellflower blooms throughout the summer. Pull away the old stems when flowering has finished.

Creeping Jenny
(*Lysimachia nummularia* 'Aurea')
One of the few plants with yellow leaves and flowers, this pretty form of creeping Jenny will quickly spread through a display and flow down the sides. As long as it is kept moist, it will grow in sun or shade.

Gourmet salad pot

Plant a container with everything you need for a delicious fresh salad. Harvest it gradually and you'll have tasty meals and a decorative pot all summer long.

Nothing beats the fresh taste of your own home-grown summer salad crops. And, with a bit of advance planning, your pots of vegetables and herbs can be pretty as well as productive. My golden rule is, if you want to keep up appearances, choose varieties that can be picked at regular intervals like parsley and non-hearting 'Lollo Rosso' lettuce. Leave out ones that are cut whole like cauliflower, or pulled like carrots, because eating them will leave an ugly gap in your container display.

There is no reason why you can't grow each variety in a pot of its own, but an eye-catching mix in a good-sized container looks more attractive. And the plants can benefit from growing up close to each other. I've put in orange-flowered tagetes (members of the marigold family) alongside the tomatoes because it will help deter whitefly.

WHEN TO PLANT – sow seeds in spring, plant in early summer

Secrets of salad success

Your salad pot will be very heavy to move once it is planted up, so put it in position before filling it. I use mine to create an eye-catching display on my patio – in a sunny spot conveniently close to my kitchen door.

It is important to take into account not only where your salad pot will look good but where the plant selection in it will be happiest. Salads need sun. Tomatoes, peppers and cucumbers will need your warmest, sunniest spot to do well. Root vegetables need sun for most of the day. Leaf crops are the only ones that won't mind growing in light, dappled shade or having sun for only part of the day, but don't try to grow them under trees or anywhere there is permanent gloom.

YOU WILL NEED

Materials and tools
- 40cm (16in) square container or a round pot of same diameter
- Chunks of broken polystyrene
- Multipurpose potting compost

Plants
Buy seeds for sowing, or buy plants as follows:
- 3 x dwarf or non-hearting lettuce ('Little Leprechaun' was my choice.)
- 2 x dwarf bush tomatoes 'Red Robin'
- 3 x orange or yellow tagetes 'Tangerine Gem' or 'Lemon Gem'
- 9 x lemon basil
- 2 x parsley plants

If you choose the same plants for your pot that I have, the best position for your container will be in full sun in a sheltered spot out of cold winds. If the best position in your garden isn't on your patio but in front of one of

1 *Sow seeds in mid spring and cover with sieved compost. To germinate, put in a heated propagator or on a windowsill indoors. After 2-3 weeks transfer the seedlings into a seed tray or into pots.*

4 *Keeping the plants in their pots, put the two tomatoes at the back with a triangle of tagetes in between. Line up the basil behind the lettuce and add the parsley plants in front of the tomatoes.*

your summer borders – don't worry. All the extra foliage and flowers in your border will add to the decorative effect and also help to disguise the vegetables from any insect pests flying overhead.

2 *Seed-grown plants will be ready to plant out in early summer, when you can also buy young plants. Cover the container base with polystyrene chunks. They help drainage and save on potting compost.*

5 *Carefully plant up your container in the planned arrangement. Ease each plant out of its pot by turning it upside down and tapping the rim of the pot to avoid disturbing the rootball.*

Bean feast

Dwarf beans come in a wonderful array of pod colours – purple, yellow and even speckled. You can grow all of them successfully in pots. Here I've made a traditional terracotta strawberry pot the centrepiece for a collection of attractive vegetables and herbs, clustering smaller pots around the base to build up the display. Nasturtiums, pot marigolds (*Calendula*) and borage will all add colour and edible flowers to your salads. Just take a look at my summer salad special at the bottom of the picture.

You will need to provide the beans with plenty of water and spray the flowers to encourage pollination. Pick them regularly or the pods will get tough and woody. If you want to, you can save bean seeds for next season. To do this just leave a few pods to ripen on the plants. I think the seeds are as fascinating and as colourful as the pods that surround them.

3 *Fill the container with compost to within 5cm (2in) of the rim. Then gather together your plants in their individual pots. Arrange the three lettuces in a line at the front of the pot to make a frilly edge.*

6 *Lightly firm in the plants, then top up with potting compost to within 2.5cm (1in) from the rim. This leaves room for watering. Give the plants a good soaking using a watering can fitted with a rose.*

IT'S HARD TO BELIEVE THAT SUCH AN ATTRACTIVE DISPLAY IS ALSO EDIBLE

Top plants for salad pots

What you want in the plants you select is flavour, the ability to keep on producing fruit, leaves or flowers all summer without going to seed, and a compact shape that doesn't need staking. An attractive appearance is also a real advantage if you want to avoid the allotment look in your garden.

The selection used in my salad pot – the dwarf bush tomato 'Red Robin', parsley, tagetes, lemon basil and the dwarf lettuce 'Little Leprechaun' – all score well for flavour and habit, as do nasturtiums, red-leaved lettuce, ruby chard and dwarf beans.

You can also grow peppers and aubergines in pots. Both, however,

must have lots of warmth and will only grow well against a south-facing wall. 'Redskin' is a good hybrid pepper for a sunny patio, and 'Mini Bambino' is a reliable aubergine to try in pots.

A great way to sample a wide range of varieties is to buy vegetables by mail order. Many are available as plug or young plant collections. Every year I like to experiment with a few different plant combinations.

AFTERCARE

Water your salad pot regularly. This will mean watering every day in hot weather, especially if the plants are mature. Apply a liquid feed each week or push in a slow-release fertilizer pellet that lasts the whole season.

Lettuce takes about 8-10 weeks to mature, so have young plants ready and waiting to replace them, or choose a non-hearting variety, with leaves you can keep on picking.

When replacing vegetables in your pot, remove all the old stems and roots and put in a double handful of fresh potting compost before adding the new plant.

Tomato 'Red Robin'
This is one of the new ultra dwarf tomatoes that can even be grown in a window box. It is more manageable than the more widely grown 'Tumbler'. Use short canes to give a little support for the weight of fruit.

Basil
For best results, delay sowing basil until late spring, then transfer the plants to 9cm (3½in) pots so they can grow to a good size before they go outside. When using, snip off young shoots just above a leaf joint to encourage new sideshoots.

Nasturtium 'Alaska Mixed'
With edible leaves, flowers and seeds, nasturtiums are the perfect addition to a collection of herbs and vegetables. They are really easy to grow, the only problem being blackfly. Nip off flower buds and leaves at the first sign of infection.

Salad leaf mixtures
Seed mixtures are being developed to supply young, tasty salad leaves that can be cut time and again. Typically they may contain lamb's lettuce, rocket, lettuce, chicory and spinach, or several lettuce varieties.

Hosta hanging display

Keep your hostas out of reach of slugs and snails by growing them in a hanging basket. This cool green planting scheme will look good from spring to the end of summer.

Hostas have stylish, distinctive and instantly recognizable leaves that are perfect as the centrepiece for a striking and unusual display. There is a vast range of hostas to choose from, with leaves varying in size from tiny to huge, and in shape from rounded to tapering. Colours vary from light to dark green, blue-grey, white, cream or gold.

For this scheme, it's best to choose two hostas with medium-sized leaves in contrasting shades. Their colours will be enhanced by the bright foliage of the golden nettle and creeping Jenny. The final result is very elegant – perfect for brightening up a shady spot, such as a dark passageway at the side of your house or corner of your patio that never gets the sun.

WHEN TO PLANT – any time from late winter to early summer

All about the basket

Hostas often end up as a backdrop to other plants – a role they are ideally suited for – but the beautifully marked and coloured leaves do deserve a more prominent position as well. So I've planted these hostas in a pretty wicker hanging basket and given them a starring role for a change. Putting your hostas high up has another bonus. It protects the leaves from slugs and snails. They just can't resist the tasty foliage and may even climb a wall and try to abseil into the hanging basket!

Smear lots of petroleum jelly on the basket and wall to stop them.

If you want to plant hostas in a container on the ground, try putting a few cloves of garlic around the roots of each hosta plant in early summer. The cloves will actually start to shoot

1 *Stand the basket on a large pot or an empty bucket to hold it steady. Apply three coats of yacht varnish inside and out, allowing it to dry between coats.*

2 *Line the basket with a bin liner and cut several slits in the base to allow water to drain away. Trim away the excess liner, leaving an overlap of about 10cm (4in).*

3 *Add a 5-8cm (2-3in) layer of poly-styrene chunks to improve drainage. This is much lighter than using stones or pieces of broken pot for drainage.*

YOU WILL NEED

Materials and tools
- Wicker hanging basket about 45cm (18in) in diameter
- Flowerpot or bucket
- Clear yacht varnish and paintbrush
- Black plastic bin liner and scissors
- Chunks of broken polystyrene
- Multipurpose potting compost

Plants
- 1 x *Hosta montana* 'Aureomarginata'
- 1 x *Hosta fortunei* var. *albopicta*
- 3 x creeping Jenny (*Lysimachia nummularia* 'Aurea')
- 3 x golden nettle (*Lamium maculatum* 'Aureum')

5 *Take the hostas out of their pots and tease out any tightly coiled roots. Plant the hostas on either side of the basket to get a balanced look. Add more compost to within 5cm (2in) of the rim.*

6 *Place the smaller plants around the edge of the basket, allowing the creeping Jenny to trail down. When you're happy with the effect, add more potting compost and firm well.*

and produce new cloves. Slugs and snails are put off by the smell.

Plant your basket from late winter through to early summer. This moisture-loving mix of plants will benefit from water-retaining gel in their compost.

4 *Half fill the basket with compost. This is a long-term planting, so it's worth using a specialist potting compost – some include water-retaining gel.*

7 *Water the basket and leave to drain. Try not to splash water directly on the hosta foliage, particularly if the sun is shining on them, as it will leave scorch marks on the leaves.*

Grasses in baskets

I like using foliage plants in my container displays. Flowers always look fabulous but it's nice to put the emphasis on leaves for a change – and this look is very fashionable at the moment, often appearing in our *Ground Force* gardens. I've filled this basket with stylish ornamental grasses and sedges. The sedge *Carex comans* 'Frosted Curls' has slender, silvery green leaves that grow to about 60cm (24in) long. The unusual curly tips make it especially pretty grown next to more upright grasses. Called variegated bird's foot sedge, *Carex ornithopoda* 'Variegata' has wider leaf blades that are pale green with a central white stripe. Completing the picture is the densely tufted ornamental grass *Festuca glauca* 'Elijah Blue' (blue fescue). It has narrow blue-grey leaves that reach about 30cm (12in) in length. Regular watering and a liquid feed like tomato fertilizer added to the water once a fortnight are all these grasses need to stay healthy. Halfway through the summer they may need tidying up. Simply pull out any leaves that have gone brown or spotty.

THESE PERENNIAL EVERGREEN PLANTS MAKE AN UNUSUAL DISPLAY

Four for foliage

The bold hosta leaves, the long trails of creeping Jenny and mounds of golden nettle mean that, first and foremost, the hosta basket is a foliage basket with the accent on leaf shape and colour – the flowers that appear in summer are a bonus. All these plants tolerate shade or partial shade and they all enjoy damp conditions so keep them well watered in summer and feed with liquid fertilizer every two or three weeks.

The plants are all fully hardy so will overwinter without the need for a greenhouse or any protection. The hostas will die back completely in late autumn, so hang the basket somewhere sheltered until they send up new shoots in spring.

AFTERCARE

This is a long-lasting combination and the plants will get better and better. However, by the end of the second year, they will probably need dividing. Empty the basket in late winter, wash it out and revarnish it. Divide all the plants and replant, using the spare plants in other containers.

Alternatively, simply remove the edging plants and leave the hostas intact. They will put on more growth the following season and soften the edge of the basket with their own foliage.

Yellow-edged hosta
(*Hosta montana* 'Aureomarginata')
The leaves of this bold hosta have dark centres with irregular pale golden edges. This is one of the first hostas to emerge in spring, which means it may suffer from brown, frost-damaged leaves. However, it usually has a second flush of leaves. In summer it also produces graceful spikes of white flowers tinged with lavender.

Golden nettle
(*Lamium maculatum* 'Aureum')
This unfussy groundcover plant forms soft mounds of foliage in a border. In a basket it will spread itself around other plants and eventually trail over the edge. It stays green for most of the year and produces small, hooded whorls of pinkish flowers in summer. Prune back any untidy growth to the base in late winter.

Wavy-edged hosta
(*Hosta fortunei var. albopicta*)
This elegant hosta has light yellow markings in the centre of its heart-shaped leaves, with irregular dark green streaking on the edges. As summer goes by, the colour contrast fades. After flowering, remove the lavender blooms.

Creeping Jenny
(*Lysimachia nummularia* 'Aurea')
A useful evergreen foliage plant, creeping Jenny will trail 20-30cm (8-12in) by the autumn and produce starry yellow flowers all along its stems. Prune back in late winter to encourage new growth.

Sweet peas for perfume

Grow pretty sweet peas in a large pot and train them round a rustic wigwam – and be sure to keep them where you can enjoy their wonderful scent.

Sweet peas are my favourite annual climbers. Their gorgeous colours and sweet perfume are great in the garden and I love picking the flowers and bringing them indoors.

If you've tried and failed with sweet peas in the past, or haven't got the ideal open, sheltered sunny bed for them, then try growing them in a roomy pot. I trained them up a rustic willow wigwam and got a stunning display.

You can put the pot in the sun right next to your favourite garden seat, or by a window where the flowers will catch your eye and the scent will drift indoors. A matching pair of pots to flank a gateway or arch like floral sentries will be a real summer delight.

WHEN TO PLANT – late spring

Planting sweet pea seedlings

You can buy sweet pea seedlings in most garden centres in late spring. I like to grow my own from seed as I get a much bigger choice of varieties that way. If you want to have a go, sow the seeds from late winter to early spring. There is no need to soak the seed before sowing. Try planting the seeds individually in plastic cell trays. That means each seedling will have its own plug of compost when you come to plant it out, so you avoid disturbing the roots. Seedlings like this will get off to a flying start. Keep the trays under glass in gentle heat.

Getting a good show

Even the most pampered sweet peas will not be able to sustain a non-stop show throughout the summer. However, by providing them with optimum growing conditions – soil enriched with organic matter, regular watering, feeding and deadheading – they should stretch into late summer.

I also stagger sowing dates to give me fresh seedlings to pop in the pot. Another tip is to slip in a seed next to each seedling as you plant. These will germinate and peak as the original seedlings are running out of steam.

YOU WILL NEED

Materials and tools
- Terracotta or wood container, 40cm (16in) in diameter
- Chunks of broken polystyrene
- Multipurpose potting compost
- Trowel
- Rustic wigwam that will fit inside rim of container, approximately 1.5m (60in) tall
- Piece of garden fleece big enough to encircle wigwam
- Clothes pegs

Plants
Grow your sweet peas from seed or buy a potful of seedlings in mixed colours – you need a minimum of 12 plants

1   *If you are using a new terracotta pot, soak it overnight – if it is not fully submerged, turn the pot so all the clay gets a soak. This prevents the pot from absorbing moisture from the potting mix.*

2   *Fill the base of the pot with a 7.5cm (3in) layer of broken chunks of polystyrene. These allow water to drain through freely without adding to the weight of the pot.*

4   *Fill the pot with compost to within 5cm (2in) of the top, then plant the seedlings around the rim. Use a trowel to make narrow planting slits, slip in the plants, then gently firm in.*

5   *Add the wigwam, pushing the uprights a few inches into the compost to anchor it – take care not to damage the delicate seedlings. Water the plants using a watering can with a rose attachment.*

Charlie says…

Match the vigour of your sweet peas to the height of your wigwam. A vigorous variety will quickly form a tangle at the top. Check the plant labels or seed packet for the expected height.

3 *Tip your seedlings out and carefully tease them apart if you've grown them in one pot. If you are buying seedlings, avoid plants that are yellow, starved or tangled at the root in an undersized pot.*

6 *Wrap the wigwam in garden fleece and secure the fleece with clothes pegs. The fabric will shelter the plants from wind and frost and give some protection from slugs and snails.*

Container climbers

Morning glory won't disappoint you if you're looking for an alternative fast-growing annual climber to grow in a container. It will climb and cling without help and produce a long-lasting show of flowers. As it reaches 3m (10ft) in height, you will need to buy a wigwam that tall or make your own with willow rods woven together with willow wands or string. Other attractive, fast-growing climbers for a large wigwam are canary creeper, with its unusual bird-shaped flowers, and the ever-popular nasturtium. Make sure you buy the climbing variety.

A MORNING GLORY (*IPOMOEA TRICOLOR* 'HEAVENLY BLUE') GROWING UP A HOMEMADE WILLOW WIGWAM

Scented heaven

The old saying that the more sweet peas you pick, the more blooms you get is absolutely true. Regular cutting will prevent seed pods from forming and encourage continued flowering. So keep picking – you'll never be short of friends and neighbours who will be delighted with a bunch of sweet peas.

Here are some of my favourite varieties of sweet pea that will do well growing in a container. And, if the bottom of your wigwam starts to look a bit bare, take my tip and add a scented companion – the geranium *Pelargonium* 'Lady Plymouth'.

AFTERCARE

Remove the garden fleece from your sweet peas after about a month.

A weekly high potash liquid feed will encourage flowering – a tomato feed is a good choice.

Spiral the sweet pea plants around the wigwam as they grow, rather than letting them grow straight up. This will encourage more flowers and keep the structure well covered.

Watch out for greenfly which start to feed on the sweet pea shoot tips and developing flowers. Dislodge them with a jet of water or spray the plants with an insecticidal soap.

Sweet pea 'Cupani'
The oldest sweet pea in cultivation, 'Cupani' was introduced to Britain in 1699. It won't give you huge blooms or long stems for cut flowers, but it does have an incredible fragrance and a long flowering period.

Sweet pea 'Galaxy Mixed'
A best-selling mixture, 'Galaxy Mixed' is vigorous and free flowering. The flowers are fragrant, and their long stems are perfect for cutting for indoor arrangements. This variety will give a good background display for more fancy varieties.

***Pelargonium* 'Lady Plymouth'**
One of the most popular of the scented-leaved geraniums, 'Lady Plymouth' makes a tough houseplant but also relishes the summer outdoors. The leaves are edged with white and smell of lemons.

Sweet pea 'Mars'
These large frilly flowers have veined and marbled markings. They have the classic sweet pea perfume and long stems. 'Nimbus' is an equally striking striped variety with blue veining.

Pond in a pot

Add a great little feature to your garden by turning a ceramic pot into a miniature pond. It's quick and easy to do and will fit into the smallest of gardens.

Water features are increasingly popular in modern gardens and obviously they are a favourite of mine, so I had to include one in this book! Using a container is one of the easiest ways to bring water into your garden and this project is suitable for even the tiniest courtyard or patio. I've used a ceramic pot, but you could just as easily use an elegant bowl, a stone trough or an old ceramic sink.

The ideal spot for this display is in full sun, but it will also work in partial shade if a sunny position is not available. Make sure it's not overhung by trees and shrubs, as falling leaves and blossom could smother it.

WHEN TO PLANT – any time after the last frosts in late spring

Pond plants explained

Pond plants are just like the rest of the plants in your garden. To grow them successfully you need to know what conditions each variety prefers. Water lilies have their roots in compost underwater, but their leaves and flowers float on the surface. Marginals also root in underwater compost, but their leaves and flowers rise above the water. Floaters move freely in the water – their roots are submerged, but not anchored, while the leaves and stems rest on the surface. Oxygenators are vital for maintaining a healthy pond but they aren't ornamental as the entire plant grows underwater. All the plants shown here are available from good water garden centres.

YOU WILL NEED

Materials and tools
- Glazed, frostproof ceramic pot, about 45cm (18in) in diameter
- Pond baskets and aquatic compost
- Gravel or pea shingle, washed
- Bricks (optional)

Plants
- 1 x water lily (*Nymphaea tetragona*)

Marginals
- 1 x *Houttuynia cordata* 'Chameleon'
- 1 x corkscrew rush (*Juncus effusus* f. *spiralis*)
- 1 x pickerel weed (*Pontederia cordata*)
- 1 x cardinal lobelia (*Lobelia cardinalis*)

Floaters
- 1 x water hyacinth (*Eichhornia crassipes*)
- 1 x water lettuce (*Pistia stratiotes*)

Oxygenators
- Three bunches (with weights) of either water milfoil (*Myriophyllum spicatum*) or hornwort (*Ceratophyllum demersum*)

1 *Thin out the houttuynia (above) and corkscrew rush by teasing apart the roots with your fingers. If the plants are pot-bound, cut them apart with a knife. It sounds brutal, but it does the plant a power of good.*

2 *Pot up the water lily and marginal plants in the baskets. Use aquatic compost or you will encourage algae. Add a top-dressing of gravel on top of the compost to anchor the pots and stop compost from leaking out.*

4 *Place the water lily at the bottom of the pot. Put the marginal plants no deeper than 10cm (4in) under the water. Use bricks or a basket full of gravel to raise the plants to the right height.*

5 *Place the water hyacinth and water lettuce in the container. These floating plants don't need a pot, they just drift about. Try not to splash the water lettuce because it will scorch in hot weather.*

Barrel of water plants

Wooden half barrels make excellent container ponds. The natural wood texture complements the water plants and the barrel provides plenty of growing space for them to thrive in. When buying your barrel look for one about 45cm (18in) in diameter and try to make sure it won't leak – if it's full of rainwater that's a good sign. If you want to use a barrel you already have, give it a clean, then fill it with water to test it. If you find it has a leak, use silicon to seal the seams and when it dries, coat the inside with a black bitu-mastic paint (available from specialist water garden centres).

Stand your barrel on a level patio, or on top of bricks in a garden border where it will blend in happily with the surrounding foliage and flowers. Stock it with water plants the same or similar to those I've chosen for the ceramic container. Don't be too enthusiastic with your planting. You should be able to see the water.

3 *Place all the plants (except for the oxygenators) on a table and organize them into an informal design. When you're happy with the arrangement, fill the glazed ceramic pot with water. Rain water is best, but tap water will do.*

6 *Attach weights around the bottom stems of oxygenating plants so they will sink to the bottom of the pot. Put the plants into the pot. These plants give off oxygen and help to keep the water clear.*

FREEZING WATER WON'T CRACK A WOODEN BARREL, BUT IT WILL DAMAGE THE PLANTS. MOVE THE POND UNDERCOVER IN VERY HARSH WINTERS

Water-loving varieties

Here is some useful extra information about most of the water-loving plants I've chosen. I also often get asked whether it is all right to put fish in these mini ponds. Fish need a well-kept pond with lots of room if they are to stay healthy so please don't try to keep them in your container – they won't thrive.

AFTERCARE

It is normal for a new pond to turn pea-soup green. As the oxygenating plants get established, the water will clear.

In the winter, floating plants normally die back and sink to the bottom of the pond, surviving as buds or seed. Other plants will need to be protected from freezing water or replaced each spring.

Water lily
(*Nymphaea tetragona*, also known as *N.* 'Pygmaea Alba')
This is the perfect water lily for a small tub. The tiny, white, star-like flowers – 2.5cm (1in) across – and small leaves, with dark green and purple undersides, die back in winter. It is fully hardy and has a spread of 45cm (18in). Plant at a depth of 30cm (12in).

Cardinal lobelia
(*Lobelia cardinalis*)
Spires of bright red flowers rise from the purplish green foliage of this fully hardy marginal plant from mid summer to autumn. Grows to 80-100cm (31-39in) tall. Plant at a depth of 0-10cm (0-4in).

Pickerel weed
(*Pontederia cordata*)
A marginal plant with glossy, heart-shaped leaves and tall spikes of blue flowers in mid to late summer. Fully hardy. Height and spread are both 60cm (23in). Plant at a depth of 0-10cm (0-4in).

***Houttuynia cordata*
'Chameleon'**
This bog/marginal plant is fully hardy but young plants are vulnerable to frost so need protecting. Height and spread are 23cm (9in) by 30cm (12in). Plant at a depth of 0-10cm (0-4in).

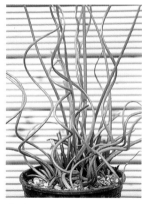

Corkscrew rush
(*Juncus effusus* f. *spiralis*)
A fully hardy marginal plant with spiralling green leaves. Divide regularly and remove leaves that grow straight. Height and spread are 45cm (18in) by 30cm (12in). Plant at a depth of 0-10cm (0-4in).

Rose and clematis barrel

Overflowing with powerful fragrance and gorgeous colour, this combination of deep pink roses and lavender-pink clematis makes a spectacular feature in the summer.

This dynamic duo – the lavender-pink clematis 'Nelly Moser' and the fragrant rose 'Gertrude Jekyll' – are ideal partners for container growing. The clematis needs something to hold on to and the rose provides the perfect robust framework. You will be thrilled by the resulting explosion of colour and fragrance.

The initial expense of the barrel container, support and two plants will definitely be worthwhile. For the following five or six years at least, you will have a glorious, overflowing container. This container will look its best in June when the first flush of clematis flowers coincides with the first flush of roses. But the 'Gertrude Jekyll' rose flowers continually over the summer so you will have colour through to the autumn.

WHEN TO PLANT – **spring**

Planting for lasting success

For a cheaper alternative to the barrel, try a plastic or glazed pot. Do not stint on size. This is a long-term planting and a large deep root run is important. Making your own wigwam from bamboo garden canes can also save you money. Bunch the canes together and secure with a plastic ring support. For a natural look, use tarred string – it does not rot and has a fabulous fragrance.

The perfect site

'Nelly Moser' is well known as a reliable, old-fashioned clematis, strong in growth and abundant in flowers. Although it has the look of an old-fashioned rose, with a multitude of petals and a sweet fragrance, the 'Gertrude Jekyll' rose is a more recent offering from plant breeders. They both enjoy shade at the roots with sunshine on the flowers. So, find a spot in the garden where, for part or most of the day, the barrel can remain cool but the top growth is bathed by sunlight. If

1 *If your barrel has no drainage holes, turn it upside down and make holes about 1cm (½in) in diameter in a circle around the base of the barrel, using a hand or electric drill.*

2 *Line the barrel with one or two black plastic bin liners. Then cut slits in the base so that excess moisture can drain away. Put in 5cm (2in) or more of broken polystyrene as drainage material.*

YOU WILL NEED

Materials and tools
- Wooden half barrel container or similar, 62.5cm (25in) diameter and 38cm (15in) deep
- Hand or power drill and large drill bit
- 1 or 2 black bin liners to line the barrel (not needed for other pots)
- Scissors
- Chunks of broken polystyrene
- Rose, tree and shrub compost
- Support – 122cm (4ft) tall cone-shaped willow frame
- Slow-release fertilizer

Plants
- 1 x *Rosa* 'Gertrude Jekyll'
- 1 x *Clematis* 'Nelly Moser'

4 *Plant the rose beside the clematis, but first add enough compost so that the top of the rose rootball sits about 5cm (2in) below the barrel rim. Leave room to put the willow frame in place without damaging the rose.*

5 *Scatter in some slow-release fertilizer and mix with the compost. Then add and firm in the compost until it reaches within 5cm (2in) of the barrel rim. Cut off the excess plastic lining and tuck in the edges below soil level.*

Something different

this isn't possible, surround the barrel with smaller pots. Plant them with foliage draping over the sides.

3   *Move the barrel to its final position before half filling it with compost. Allow enough room to plant the clematis 15cm (6in) below the rim and put it about 10cm (4in) from the edge of the barrel.*

I like the rose and clematis combination so much that I tried out this alternative planting scheme using another pink, scented, repeat-flowering shrubby rose called 'Armada' and the blue 'The President' clematis. Instead of a willow frame, I used a cheaper metal cone-shaped support. And I picked a large blue-glazed pot to complement the colours of the flowers.

If you want to try this variation, follow the same planting procedure but omit the plastic lining. Before inserting the frame, tie string around the rose stems to make the plant more compact. Once the support is firmly positioned, cut the string. The rose will soon make new outward growth and take on a good shape.

6   *Remove any cane supports tied to the plants. Then place the willow frame over the plants and push it firmly down into the compost. To encourage flowering at the base, bring the clematis around the bottom of the frame. Water well.*

Charlie says...

After a few years the clematis can become unbalanced, with all the new growth at the top and bare stems at the bottom. To prevent this, immediately after the first flush of flowers in early summer, prune a few of the main stems back to within a couple of

inches of the base. This will encourage new growth at the bottom of the plant and this growth will produce flowers low down the following year. Each spring, before new growth starts, cut out dead stems and prune back to strong leaf buds.

Dynamic duos

The *Rosa* 'Gertrude Jekyll' and *Clematis* 'Nelly Moser' make an irresistible combination. The scrolled buds on the 'Gertrude Jekyll' open to reveal an abundance of rich, deep pink petals. These blooms are so strongly scented that they will fill your whole patio with a delicious old-fashioned rose perfume. 'Nelly Moser' comes into flower before the rose, with masses of lavender-pink blooms, each petal with a central darker carmine stripe. As the flowers of this rose and clematis age, they fade into a lovely, soft pastel pink.

For a dramatic pink and blue pairing, plant *Rosa* 'Armada' and *Clematis* 'The President' together. It makes a great garden-warming gift!

Rosa 'Gertrude Jekyll'
Bred by David Austen as recently as 1986, this rose is prized for its old-fashioned appearance and its ability to repeat-flower throughout the summer and autumn. Its flowers have plenty of deep pink petals and a generous scent. A healthy, vigorous shrubby rose, it grows to about 1.2m (4ft) tall with a spread of 1m (3ft).

Clematis 'Nelly Moser'
An old favourite amongst clematis for its vigour and sheer quantity of blooms, Clematis 'Nelly Moser' grows to 2.5-3m (7.5-9ft) in height. Its flowers, which appear in early summer, are 12-16cm (5-6½in) wide. The lavender-pink shadings on the petals make this plant a good companion for a pink or white rose.

AFTERCARE

It is vital that your clematis does not dry out. During the spring and summer, it will need watering daily. Adding a mulch over the compost will help retain water.

Apply a general-purpose rose feed to the barrel in March or April, then again towards the end of June, after the first main flush of flowers. During the main flowering periods, give the plants weekly applications of a liquid fertilizer.

At the end of June and early July, trim off any dead heads on the rose back to about 8cm (3in) of the stem. Remove dead wood in February or March and lightly prune to maintain a good shape. See page 79 for clematis pruning tips.

Rosa 'Armada'
Introduced in 1988 by Harkness Roses, *Rosa* 'Armada' is a vigorous, healthy and reliable free-branching shrub rose that grows to about 1.35m (4½ft) tall and wide. It produces sprays of strongly spice-scented deep pink flowers that are about 8cm (3in) across and has plenty of glossy, deep green leaves.

Clematis 'The President'
Producing masses of single, rich purple-blue flowers with a silver sheen beneath, *Clematis* 'The President' grows to 2-3m (6-9ft). The flowers are 10cm (4in) wide and have red anthers. The generous height of 'The President' means that it can successfully be trained sideways, giving you lots of flowers at all levels.

Climbers with trellis

Put up some trellis, pop a colourful climber in a container underneath it and, hey presto, you have a magic way to brighten up a boring wall.

If you want to hide a boring bare shed or boundary wall with a climbing plant but the ground underneath is covered with concrete – don't despair. You can grow your climber in a pot. Look for a striking climber that will go on for years, such as this ceanothus (*Ceanothus* 'Concha') or the white clematis (*Clematis* 'Guernsey Cream') on page 83. Both grow well in pots and produce eye-catching displays of blooms. In fact, they will become a major feature in your garden. Don't try to subdue the show-stopping nature of these climbers – it's much better to encourage it by painting the wall behind the plant in an attention-grabbing colour or positioning the container display where nothing else competes with it.

WHEN TO PLANT – early spring or autumn

Fixing trellis to a wooden wall

Buy a fan-shaped trellis for your container climber. You can train the plant to take on the same shape and it will look as if a bouquet of flowers is growing in your container. Follow my simple fixing instructions to make sure your climber will be safely and attractively secured to your wall.

Once the trellis is up, plant the grouping in early spring.

Simple carpentry

Only the most basic carpentry skills are needed to put up your trellis, but you might like to have someone else on hand to assist you. Then, while your trellis is held temporarily in place, you can stand back to decide if it looks right. It's certainly not worth buying tools or a workbench specially for this little job, so if you

1 *Drill a fixing hole at the top and bottom of the two outermost verticals of the trellis. Put the pot in place and hold the trellis above it. Mark the wall through the holes with a bradawl. Remove the trellis and drill pilot holes in the wall.*

2 *For spacers, cut four 38mm lengths of 20mm by 20mm hardwood. These are needed to hold the trellis away from the wall. This allows air to circulate behind your plant, keeping it healthy and allowing it to wind around the trellis.*

4 *Holding the spacers between the trellis and the wooden wall, fix the trellis to the wall with 65mm No 8 screws. Screw through the trellis fixing holes and the spacers and into the wall.*

5 *Place some crocks in the bottom of the container. Then fill with compost, mixing in some slow-release fertilizer. Plant your climber so that it is angled back towards the trellis.*

Fixing trellis to a brick wall

don't have the few tools you need, hire them for the weekend. Check your wall before beginning to see if there is any danger of drilling into an electric cable or a water pipe.

Clematis is ideal for softening the hard look of a bare brick wall, and the 'Guernsey Cream' I've chosen for the display below is particularly effective. The underplanting of heuchera and purple sage will keep the clematis roots shaded just the way they like it. It's best to plant this arrangement in the autumn to give it a chance to get well established before the growing season the following spring. Put it in a sunny spot and, in winter, protect the container with garden fleece or move it into a conservatory if it isn't too heavy. Before you start attaching trellis to a brick wall, check that the mortar is sound. Repoint if necessary and allow the mortar to dry out before drilling any holes.

3   *Securely clamp each spacer to the workbench or table. Then, using a drill bit large enough to take the screw you will be using to fix the spacer to the wall, drill a hole right the way down the centre of the spacer.*

1   *Mark the positions for the trellis fixings on the wall (see Step 1 on the left). Then drill holes in the brick wall and tap in wall plugs with a hammer.*

6   *Tie your climber to the trellis with string. Then add the companion plants to the front of the container and firm in. Water well. Tie in new shoots as they appear, and loosen old ties if necessary.*

2   *Make four spacers (see Steps 2 and 3 on the left). With spacers between the wall and trellis, attach the trellis with 65mm screws.*

Climbers and companions

The long-flowering climbers – ceanothus and clematis – are top of my list when it comes to choosing perennial climbers to grow in containers. You will want your climbers to look good for several years so it's best to use a soil-based potting compost and to choose a sturdy, attractive container. I think terracotta always looks good and you can buy big pots quite cheaply. Check that your pot is guaranteed frost-proof.

I recommend putting some low-growing or trailing plants in the pot under the climber. These plants will add interest and colour, protect and shelter the climber's roots and cover the base of the climber if it gets a bit bare and straggly. You can renew these plants each season if you like.

I've chosen osteospermum and ivy to go with the ceanothus, and purple sage and heuchera to complement the clematis display. If you want to use other companions for your ceanothus or clematis, pick plants with colourful flowers and go for foliage with interesting leaf shapes and textures. It's also important to choose plants of similar vigour otherwise one plant will take over and dominate the display.

Osteospermum
Happy in bright sunshine, this pretty 'daisy' will flower all summer given good drainage and a sheltered site. It's best treated as an annual and replaced each year. It grows to about 45cm (18in).

Variegated ivy (*Hedera*)
Choose ivies with leaves edged in silver for the ceanothus display. Variegated ivy keeps its colour best in sun but isn't fussy about the soil it is grown in. Its shoots will trail to about 60cm (2ft) or more.

AFTERCARE

Keep your planter well watered, and each spring push slow-release fertilizer pellets into the compost.

Deadhead osteospermums and heuchera, but leave clematis flowers for their attractive seedheads.

Prune ceanothus after flowering to keep it in shape, and cut back the ivy if it gets too long and straggly. Tidy the clematis in late winter by cutting back some of the old shoots. The sage can be trimmed if necessary. Divide the clumps of heuchera if they get too big.

Ceanothus 'Concha'
Smothered in tight clusters of dark blue flowers, this evergreen is an arresting sight in early summer. It can grow to about 3m (10ft) and needs the shelter of a sunny wall.

Clematis 'Guernsey Cream'
The creamy white of these flowers is an unusual colour for a clematis. 'Guernsey Cream' will flower in early summer and again later in the year if well fed. It grows to about 2.5m (8ft) high.

Daisies on display

For a super long-lasting container display that starts in mid summer and goes on until the first frost, try my combination of daisies and silver and blue foliage.

The daisy family includes a lot of very popular flowers – from the tiny ones I loved to pick as a child to make into daisy chains to huge golden sunflowers. Coneflowers (*Rudbeckia* and *Echinacea*), strawflowers (*Helichrysum*) and asters also belong to this big and colourful group. What all these flowers have in common is the flat or cone-shaped centre that gives them the typical 'daisy' look.

Plants in the daisy family tend to have lots of long-lasting flowers, so they are ideal for containers. This display features two types of rudbeckia and a strawflower. The blue grass and silver senecio foliage at the base add contrast and a touch of sophistication.

WHEN TO PLANT – sow seeds in early spring, plant container in late spring

Success with seeds

Rudbeckia and strawflowers are not easy to get hold of as plants, so I raise mine from seed. A bit more work perhaps, but it saves money and gives me lots of plants left over to swop or give to friends. If you grow more daisies than you need for your container display, plant them in a border. They are useful space fillers and pretty flowers for picking and bringing indoors. You can also dry strawflowers for indoor displays – cut them when the petals are still curved in and hang them upside down in bunches in a dry, airy place.

Growing from seed

You need to sow a whole packet of rudbeckia seeds and about half a packet of strawflower seeds to get a really stunning display. Sow and grow the seeds on as explained in the steps below. Put the heated propagator and the seedling trays on a windowsill indoors, or in a greenhouse, porch or conservatory. They need plenty of light to do well.

Dusty miller (*Senecio*) can also be grown from seed, but it is rather slow growing, so I usually buy young plants in the spring.

Choose a position for your display in full sun. It's easiest to plant the pot up in position – full of compost and plants it will be heavy to move. Bear in mind that containers don't have to sit on paving – I put this one in a plain border to add colour. In the right position and deadheaded regularly, the daisies will reward you with a continual display of flowers from mid summer until the first frosts.

YOU WILL NEED

Materials and tools
- Propagator, seed trays, labels and 13cm (5in) plastic pots
- Large pot, 50cm (20in) in diameter
- Chunks of broken polystyrene
- Multipurpose potting compost
- Plastic plant labels

Seeds and plants
- 1 x packet of *Rudbeckia* 'Becky Mixed' seeds (to grow 10 cone flower plants)
- 1 x packet of *Rudbeckia* 'Sonora' seeds (to grow 12 coneflower plants)
- 1 x packet of *Helichrysum* 'Bright Bikini Mixed' seeds (to grow 20 strawflower plants)
- 3 x blue fescue (*Festuca glauca*)
- 4 x dusty miller (*Senecio cineraria* 'White Diamond')

1 *Sow your rudbeckia and strawflower seeds in a single seed tray in early spring. Use plant labels as dividers between the three different flowers. Cover the seeds with a sprinkling of compost and water. Put the tray in a heated propagator.*

2 *When the seedlings are large enough to handle, transfer them to other seed trays, about 32 to a tray. Handle them carefully – by the leaves not by the stems. Keep the seedlings at a minimum temperature of 10°C (50°F).*

3 *Buy young dusty miller (*Senecio*) plants in the spring. They will be widely available. For bumper-sized plants, transfer the young plants to 13cm (5in) pots and grow them on until you're ready to add them to your display.*

Charlie's choice

No other blooms are quite as fresh and appealing as crisp white daisies. In the right container a mass of white marguerites (*Argyranthemum frutescens*) will look at home in just about any style and size of garden. These daisy-like flowers are ideal for growing in a big pot on a sunny patio and will produce long-lasting blooms from early summer onwards.

Another white daisy that I think is a real winner is the shasta daisy (*Leucanthemum* x *superbum* 'Wirral Supreme') – it's easy to grow and has bright white flowers which look good in the garden and make long-lasting cut flowers. Like all daisies it flowers like mad from July through to September. Shasta daisies, especially the dwarf varieties, are well suited to growing in containers. Try the dwarf variety 'Snow Lady', which has single white flowers and only reaches about 40cm (16in), or the 30cm (12in) tall 'Silberprinzesschen' and 'Snowcap'. A shasta daisy will last two to three years before out-growing a pot and looks great mixed with colourful trailing annuals such as lobelia.

4 *In mid spring, transfer some of the rudbeckia and strawflower plants from the trays into 13cm (5in) pots. Force these on under cover so they will grow into bushy plants that will flower a couple of weeks earlier than those in the trays.*

5 *In late spring, plant up your display. Put some chunks of polystyrene in the bottom of the pot for drainage and then add the compost. Plant the blue fescue at the front edge of the pot and two groups of two senecios between them.*

6 *Add 20 young strawflower plants, and 22 of the two types of rudbeckia. Make sure you keep plenty of compost around the roots. Concentrate the dwarf 'Becky Mixed' at the front and intermix the other two daisies behind.*

Delightful daisies

There is no doubt that if it's bright and cheerful summer colour you're looking for, then daisies are an excellent choice. They look at home in traditional gardens and in modern settings, too. Here are profiles of the daisies I chose for my display, as well as an extra dwarf sunflower that I really recommend you get to know and grow. You may only be aware of the huge giant sunflowers but there are now some great varieties that will be quite at home in your containers and window boxes.

Keep an eye on your young rudbeckia plants. They are prone to grey mould disease which can spread from the leaves to attack the stems, particularly in cold, damp conditions. Remove the lower leaves as soon as they show any signs of turning yellow.

AFTERCARE

Water your daisy display regularly and use slow-release fertilizer pellets.

In windy sites, tall rudbeckias can be blown down. If necessary support your 'Sonora' with pea sticks.

Leave the daisy pot untouched in winter and allow the stems and flowers to dry off and skeletonize – they look pretty when touched with frost. In a mild winter, the senecio will survive unscathed and the blue fescue can be kept as a permanent edging in the pot.

Coneflower
(*Rudbeckia hirta* 'Sonora')
This is perhaps the most spectacular of all the coneflowers. The yellow petals are stained mahogany in the centre. Like all rudbeckias, 'Sonora' is extremely rain resistant and makes an excellent cut flower. It grows to 30-38cm (12-15in) tall and may need staking.

Coneflower
(*Rudbeckia hirta* 'Becky Mixed')
Along with 'Toto', this is the shortest rudbeckia and is only about 25cm (10in) tall, which makes it suitable for window boxes or even hanging baskets. The flowers, often with red and brown centres, vary from bright yellow to golden orange. Mine all turned out to be yellow.

Strawflower
(*Helichrysum* 'Bright Bikini Mixed')
This easy-to-grow hardy annual with papery flowers will bring brilliant colour to any sunny spot in your garden. It grows to 38cm (15in) tall. Watch out for slugs, as they love its lush green leaves.

Sunflower
(*Helianthus annuus* 'Big Smile')
There are sunflowers to suit every size of pot, from the knee-high 'Teddy Bear' to the massive 'Russian Giant'. 'Big Smile' is a lovely dwarf. Its blooms are 15cm (6in) across and it grows to 38cm (15in) tall.

Jungle plants

Give your garden a tropical feel with pots full of large-leaved plants. Group them together to make a mini jungle or put individual pots in your borders to fill gaps and add interest.

Large leaves give a tropical feel to a plant and in order to achieve them you need year-round heat and plenty of water. I love this luxuriant look, so as I don't live in a tropical climate, I've worked out my own way of getting a jungle effect. What my simulated large-leaved plants need is an early start – to give them a longer growing season – and regular watering. This makes them perfect candidates for container growing.

The tropical feel is perfect for many of our modern *Ground Force* gardens, so try them yourself if you want a contemporary look. You can pot up your jungle, then provide a little warmth and protection from spring frosts, to get the plants growing before the summer even arrives. By late summer you'll be amazed by the size and luxuriance many will have achieved.

Potting up the jungle plants

The big, bold leaves in my mini jungle are those of ginger lily, banana, canna, ruby chard and the foxglove tree. The exotic leaves and cane-like stems of the ginger lily make it a must-have for a container jungle. A tender perennial, it comes into growth in spring time, and as an added bonus, it bears beautiful fragrant lemon-yellow flowers in late summer. I've also included the fast-growing, half-hardy castor oil plant. It carries on the deep reddish theme in its bronze leaves and adds variety to the array of leaf shapes. To grow a castor oil plant from seed, sow several seeds directly into a pot and thin to leave the best single seedling. Keep it frost free until it's ready to join your display.

Although several of the 'jungle' plants I've selected are tropical, not all are. I chose the hardy plants – the gum tree, foxglove tree and ruby chard – because their leaf size and colour add to the jungle effect. The gum tree (*Eucalyptus*) provides extra height at the back as well as more

1   *Before planting your jungle plants in pots, mix water-retaining gel in the multipurpose potting compost to help prevent the compost from drying out.*

2   *In early spring, plant each of the canna rhizomes in its own pot. Pot each of the other plants in its own pot. Plant the seeds (see 'Charlie says', opposite).*

3   *Keep the Japanese banana, cannas and ginger lily protected from frost (see page 22). Also protect them from slugs and snails – a bite through young rolled canna leaves will cause damage like this.*

4   *In late spring, once there is no danger of frost, arrange the plants outside in their pots to create a jungle effect. To bring out the best deep leaf colours, place in full sun.*

YOU WILL NEED

Materials and tools
- Water-retaining gel
- Multipurpose potting compost
- Plastic and terracotta pots
- General-purpose liquid feed

Plants
- 1 x small foxglove tree (*Paulownia tomentosa*)
- 1 x small gum tree (*Eucalyptus pauciflora* subsp. *debeuzevillei*)
- 1 x Japanese banana (*Musa basjoo*)
- 1 x small ginger lily (*Hedychium gardnerianum*)

Rhizomes
- 3 x *Canna* 'Black Knight'
- 3 x *Canna* 'King Humbert'
- 3 x *Canna* 'Wyoming'

Seeds
- Castor oil plant (*Ricinus communis* 'Carmencita' or 'Gibsonii')
- Ruby chard

Welcoming hot pots

contrast in colour and leaf size.

To grow ruby chard, sow the seeds straight into a pot and thin out to three plants. Since this ornamental vegetable is hardy, you can grow it on outdoors.

Pot up your mini jungle in plastic pots rather than terracotta ones. Compost loses moisture more slowly inside a plastic pot than inside porous terracotta. The plants will also be easier to move about in light-weight plastic pots. When the plants are ready to go on show outside, I check which containers will be easily seen and, for these plants, I pop the plastic pot inside a bigger, more attractive terracotta container.

Charlie says...

The seeds of castor oil are poisonous. Although the plant is grown primarily for foliage, flowers are produced during the summer and are quickly followed by attractive spiny seeds. Collect the seed at the end of the season. Remove and discard the poisonous spiny seed coat and store the beans inside a sealed paper envelope. Label and keep cool and dry for planting next year.

The red flowers in my display really add heat to the jungle theme. Some gardeners avoid brightly coloured flowers because they can be overwhelming – but if you do, you're really missing out. Hot colours are invigorating, bright and warming. I particularly like brightly coloured plants at the entrance to my house and garden where they provide a really warm welcome for my visitors.

Choose your plants carefully as not all reds mix well together. My hot display below avoids any blue-reds or purple-reds, and uses scarlet-reds. Plus I've added plants with a bit of mahogany and orange. It includes two marigolds, 'Disco Red' and 'Red Gem', plus ruby chard, *Papaver* 'Ladybird', *Nasturtium* 'Gleaming Mahogany', *Fuchsia* 'Thalia', *Lotus berthelotii*, *Arctotis* 'Red Devil', *Dahlia* 'Bishop of Llandaff', *Lilium* 'Corina' and red busy lizzie. Each plant has its own pot. This means I can shuffle the pots around to make the best arrangement – depending on which plants look best at the time.

A CHEERING SUMMER DISPLAY OF HOT REDS AND ORANGES

Getting the luxuriant look

I love cannas – that's why I planted up nine for my display! Cannas are tropical plants that grow from a rhizome, and they have very attractive foliage and flowers. The large, deep red-brown leaves spiral gracefully up the stem. Appearing towards the end of the summer, the exotic flowers are held at the top of erect stems 60-90cm (2–3ft) tall. The dramatic red flowers of 'Black Knight' grace my display, but the rich tangerine blooms of the hybrid 'Wyoming' would also look good in a mini jungle planting scheme. A canna in a pot is also an ideal filler for a gap at the back of your summer border. If you come across any other plants with a jungle-look or with brightly coloured flowers which have a hot, tropical feel, don't hesitate to add them to your display. You can keep your mini jungle display looking fresh and interesting all summer by moving the pots around to show-off the plants looking at their best and by adding new plants. Look out for suitable candidates at your garden centre in late spring and early summer.

AFTERCARE

Once you have moved your jungle plants outdoors, water them well and feed them weekly with a general-purpose liquid feed to fuel their growth.

Cannas can be saved for next year. In autumn, allow the plants to die down and the pots to dry off. Remove the compost and store the rhizomes in peat, sand or wood shavings kept just very slightly moist. Your plants will grow to twice the size the next year!

Overwinter ginger and banana plants in their pots in the house or conservatory – you might have to cut the stems down to near compost level if you haven't the space and light to keep them in growth.

Canna 'Wyoming'
The dark, almost purple leaves of this canna form the backdrop for rich frilly tangerine blooms marked with apricot splashes and darker edges.

Canna 'Black Knight'
Bold bronze leaves are complemented by dramatic deep red, wavy-edged flowers similar to gladioli, which can last from mid summer to the first frosts.

Banana
(*Musa basjoo*)
This evergreen perennial with large tropical-looking leaves is normally grown in a conservatory, but it will grow outside during the summer.

Foxglove tree
(*Paulownia tomentosa*)
This is a hardy deciduous tree which is grown for its huge plate-like leaves which get bigger each year if the tree is pruned annually.

Strawberry tower

For a delicious display of strawberries grow them in a traditional terracotta strawberry pot with side planting pockets. I fitted my pot with its own watering system.

Freshly picked strawberries have a flavour all of their own. Grown in a bed in the garden they take up lots of space and need a good deal of care, but they can also be produced successfully in containers. Not only will the plants give an enjoyable crop of fruit, but there will also be flowers which are pretty and decorative, so there is a long season of interest.

If you're serious about getting a reasonable crop from your container, you'll need a large one. The traditional terracotta or stoneware 'strawberry pot' with side planting pockets is the best, but you can also use a large wooden half barrel or a terracotta pot of a similar size. There's nothing stopping you using strawberry plants for purely decorative purposes – both the flowers and berries look stunning spilling out of a hanging basket or a wall pot.

WHEN TO PLANT – **early spring or late summer to early autumn**

Buying and planting strawberries

To make sure that my thirsty strawberries never dry out, I've made a special plastic watering tube for my strawberry pot. It runs down the centre of the container making sure all the plants get plenty of water.

Follow the steps below to make one for your strawberry pot.

Plant perpetual-fruiting varieties of strawberry in spring and others in middle to late summer or early autumn – they'll fruit the following year. Cover the top of the compost with grit. It helps to keep the moisture in and the slugs and snails out.

Strawberry plants do best in full sun, so choose a sunny spot that also has some protection from the wind.

YOU WILL NEED

Materials and tools
- Terracotta strawberry pot, about 27cm (10½in) in diameter and 45cm (18in) tall
- Terracotta pot feet
- Broken crocks and horticultural grit
- 70mm (2¾in) black rainwater pipe taller than your pot
- Wood batten and chalk
- Hack saw
- Drill and 8mm drill bit
- Black duct tape
- Multipurpose potting compost
- Slow-release granular fertilizer

Plants
- Strawberry plants – 1 for each opening and 4 for the top (see page 96 for plant varieties)

Charlie says…

You can also grow your strawberries in 'purpose-built' plastic pot towers – they're not as pretty as the traditional strawberry pots, but they have a built-in watering system – and if you want to grow a bigger crop they'll save you the expense of buying lots of large terracotta towers.

1 *Put your pot where you want it to stand. Then put pot feet under it to promote air circulation and good drainage. Cover the drainage hole with a layer of broken crocks.*

2 *To further aid drainage, add a layer of horticultural grit about 2cm (¾in) thick on top of the broken crocks. Strawberries like moist compost, but good drainage is essential for healthy plants.*

5 *Seal one end of the pipe with duct tape, so that when water is poured in, it will fill the pipe up to the top before draining through the drilled holes. Put the pipe, open end up, in the centre of the pot.*

6 *Holding the pipe steady, fill the pot with compost to the first set of openings. Mix in slow-release fertilizer as you go. Push one plant through each opening from the outside and spread out the roots.*

Buying strawberry plants

You may be able to get strawberry plants from your local garden centre, but it is a good idea to buy them from a specialist grower – to ensure that they're virus- and disease-free. Buy healthy-looking young plants with lots of light-coloured roots and make your choice of variety carefully, weighing the quality of the flavour against the disease-resistance. Consider the cropping time as well, since different varieties will bear fruit at different times in the summer and autumn.

If your aim is mainly to have an attention-grabbing display, look for unusual strawberry plants – like pink-flowered ones, or those with pink or yellow fruit.

Herb display

After two or three years you will need to replace the strawberry plants in your pot. If you are ready for a change you'll find that a traditional strawberry pot makes an attractive and practical home for many types of plant. Fresh herbs look wonderful in a strawberry pot. Plant one up with culinary herbs and keep it near your kitchen door. The watering system will be a boon for the herbs growing low down in the pot, but avoid overwatering as too much water can cause just as much trouble as too little (See pages 39–42 for more about herbs.)

3   Stand a 70mm (2 ¾in) rainwater pipe in the centre of the pot. Then put a batten across the top of the pot and use it to help you draw a chalk mark around the pipe, level with the top of the pot.

4   Take the pipe out of the pot, and use a hack saw to cut off the excess along the chalk line. Then, using an 8mm drill bit, carefully drill drainage holes at regular intervals all down and around the pipe.

7   Firm in the first set of plants, then fill with compost up to the next set of openings, again mixing in fertilizer. Add the next set of plants and repeat this until you reach the top.

8   Put four plants around the top of the pot, firm in, then cover the compost with horticultural grit. Water thoroughly, filling the plastic pipe a few times and pouring in water on top of the grit as well.

Strawberry selection

Grow several pots of different strawberries and you can have constant crops from mid summer through into autumn. There are three types of strawberries (*Fragaria*) to choose from – summer-fruiting, perpetual-fruiting and alpine. Summer-fruiting varieties are the most popular, give the largest fruit and provide a single crop. Perpetual-fruiting varieties bear slightly smaller fruit but can crop twice in one year. The third type of strawberry is called 'alpine' or 'wild'. Alpines grow very small but delicious fruit and have a productive life of only one year, unlike summer-fruiters which will give good crops for three to four years, and perpetuals which are productive for two years. If you want the distinctive alpine strawberry flavour in a bigger berry, try the summer-fruiting 'Rosie'. Two other good summer-fruiters are the very popular 'Cambridge Favourite' and 'Hapil'. For one of the tastiest perpetual-fruiters, try 'Challenger'.

AFTERCARE

Water your strawberry pot regularly and thoroughly to keep the compost moist, but avoid watering late in the day.

If you didn't put slow-release fertilizer in the pot, give the plants a liquid feed once every week during flowering and fruiting.

Over winter, keep the pot in a light spot that is protected from frost if possible. Alternatively, trim back all the foliage and cover the plant crowns with straw.

Pinch off strawberry runners to keep your pot looking neat. After two or three years, depending on the type of strawberry (see above), remove the contents of the pot and discard the plants. Clean the pot and replant.

Mara des Bois
The fruit of this perpetual-fruiting variety is intensely red when ripe and the flavour is excellent. Resistant to powdery mildew, the plant gives a good crop from late summer through to mid autumn.

Rosie
A summer-fruiting variety, 'Rosie' produces a crop that is ready in mid June to mid July. The glossy berries are dark red and have an excellent flavour similar to that of alpine varieties.

A touch of the Orient

This vibrant combination of plants in a lacquer-look container will bring a taste of the Orient to your garden. Decorate your own pot for a truly unique display.

One interesting container full of unusual plants can bring an instant new look to an empty spot on your decking or patio – especially if you add some other appropriate accessories like pebbles, cushions or lanterns for a special occasion.

The planting scheme for this oriental-style display is one of foliage contrasts. The painted ferns (*Athyrium niponicum* var. *pictum*) add fullness and will soften the edge of the pot. The grasses will flower, but with understated elegance rather than spectacular colour. And the sacred bamboo (*Nandina domestica*), which also flowers in summer, will steal the show in autumn when its leaves change to a stunning shade of red.

Vibrant plants like these need a striking container to set them off. I've decorated a terracotta pot to create my very own unique planter.

A quick word of warning for those with children, the berries of the sacred bamboo are poisonous, so make sure that you place the container where it's safely out of reach of both children and pets.

WHEN TO PLANT – **spring or autumn**

Lacquering the pot

Follow these simple steps to convert a bell-shaped terracotta pot into the perfect container for my oriental-style display. The leaf motifs on the pot should be large enough to stand out boldly, but only put a few around the pot to keep the design simple. If you find it difficult to trace around your leaf on to the paper below, lay a piece of tracing paper on top and trace the shape on to it instead, then trace this outline on to the thin paper.

YOU WILL NEED

Materials and tools
- PVA glue and paintbrush
- Frost-proof terracotta bell pot, 41cm (16in) in diameter
- Matt emulsion (aubergine colour)
- 3 x pot feet
- Selection of leaves
- Thin paper, pencil and craft knife
- Stencil mount spray adhesive
- Stencil brush
- Bronze metallic paint (any kind)
- Oil-based gloss varnish
- Wet and dry fine-grade abrasive paper
- Soft, dry cloth
- Broken crocks
- Multipurpose potting compost

Plants
- 1 x sacred bamboo (*Nandina domestica*)
- 2 x Japanese bloodgrass (*Imperata cylindrica* 'Red Baron')
- 1 x Hakone grass (*Hakonechloa macra* 'Aureola')
- 2 x Japanese painted fern (*Athyrium niponicum* var. *pictum*)

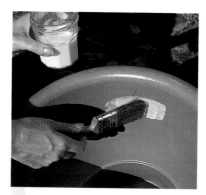

2 *Select one leaf, or use a selection in different shapes and sizes. On a thin piece of paper, draw around the outline of your leaf or leaves and pencil in the major veins. Using a craft knife, cut out the areas between the outline and the veins to give a free, open pattern. If you don't add any veins, your leaves may end up as unrecognizable solid blobs.*

1 *Mix one part PVA to three parts water. Paint the inside (not the outside) of the pot and the base to seal out moisture and prevent the paint from discolouring. Once the sealant is dry, paint the outside of the pot and the top 10cm (4in) inside with matt emulsion. Leave to dry. Give the pot a second coat. Paint the pot feet – there's no need to seal them with PVA.*

3 *Spray the stencil with stencil mount and press it on to the pot. Don't worry if the stencil wrinkles – just make sure that the leaf outline is in direct contact with the pot, or the paint may run under the stencil. Dip the stencil brush in bronze paint, blot off most of the paint, then stipple paint over the stencil. While the paint is still moist, remove the stencil.*

4 *When the bronze paint is dry, apply a thin coat of varnish to the whole pot. When that is dry, dip the abrasive paper into water and rub lightly over the pot to smooth the surface – a milky residue will appear. Wipe clean with a soft, dry cloth, then varnish and sand two or three times. The more layers of varnish, the richer the finish will be. Don't sand the final layer.*

Japanese companions

All the plants in this arrangement are originally from Japan, but don't worry – they are available from most garden centres.

After the varnish on your pot has completely dried, position it where you want it to stand – for best results, place it in partial shade. Put the pot feet underneath. Add broken crocks in the bottom for drainage, then half fill the pot with multipurpose potting compost. Plant the sacred bamboo at the back of the pot, one bloodgrass in the middle and one on the right, and the Hakone grass on the left. Position the fern at the front to soften the front rim. Top up with compost and firm in. Water the container well after planting.

Charlie says...

Try painting the pot feet the same colour as the stencil. It will give balance to the colour scheme.

Prevent frost damage by lining the pot with bubble wrap before adding the compost. Cut holes in the wrap to allow for drainage.

Bear in mind the gloss on this pot is a varnish and not a glaze. Although it is quite tough, it's not as durable as a fired glaze. Treat it with some care and try not to rub the sides against any hard surfaces.

AFTERCARE

Each spring, sprinkle a little blood, fish and bone over the surface of the compost. During warm weather, water well and do not let the compost dry out.

All the plants should survive the winter unless the temperature drops below -15°C (5°F), in which case, move the pot into a frost-free conservatory, greenhouse or porch.

The plants in this container will grow well together for a couple of seasons with little maintenance. When they outgrow their space, plant them in your garden.

Mulching the surface of the compost with fine bark chips will help retain moisture and looks attractive.

Sacred bamboo
(*Nandina domestica*)
This trouble-free, evergreen, bamboo-like shrub has everything – young, red foliage, white flowers in mid summer and autumn berries if the weather has been warm. After five years' growth it's still a manageable 1m (39in). Its ultimate size is 2m (6½ft).

Hakone grass
(*Hakonechloa macra* 'Aureola')
This grass has arching golden and green striped leaves throughout the growing season, with delicate bronze flower spikes in late summer. The leaves colour best in partial shade and become reddish in autumn. It likes a moist, humus-rich soil.

Japanese painted fern
(*Athyrium niponicum* var. *pictum*)
A slightly unusual and graceful fern with maroon leaf stalks. Likes some shade and soil that doesn't dry out. Its grey-green foliage contrasts well with bright-coloured grasses. It isn't evergreen but fresh fronds reappear each spring.

Japanese bloodgrass
(*Imperata cylindrica* 'Red Baron')
The leaves of this eye-catcher turn an impressive crimson as the summer progresses. A native of Japan, it likes moisture-retentive soil, in sun or part shade. Ideal for using in a container, it grows no taller then 50cm (20in).

Autumn and winter

Brighten up autumn and winter

In most parts of the country, summer window boxes and tubs will carry on flowering well into October, but they are usually past their best several weeks before that. And once the first frost hits them many plants will be reduced to the consistency of wet tissue paper. I prefer to dismantle my summer containers in late September and change my colour scheme with the season. Don't give up on containers – or the garden for that matter – just because winter's on the way. Take the opportunity to try new colour schemes and plant combinations, and surround the house with a warm overcoat of glowing evergreens, berries, coloured stems and flowers too – planted up in frost-proof containers of course.

Autumn leaf colour can be simply spectacular and Japanese maples in a front garden in October never fail to entrance passers-by with their characteristic bonfire tints. *Skimmia* 'Rubella' is another plant I wouldn't be without. It straddles three seasons, the fat red buds of autumn and winter finally opening in April. Planted alongside the vivid purples and pinks of ornamental cabbages and kales, this neat little shrub takes on a new dimension, and more traditionally planted with dwarf chrysanthemums (especially from the American-bred Yoder series), it sparkles.

Once the sun is low in the sky heralding colder weather it's time to reserve your sunniest, most sheltered spot for your favourite winter arrangement and group other containers together near windows. There they can be seen from indoors when the weather's only fit for armchair gardening! Pots arranged in groups not only look good but provide mutual protection.

Don't think of this time of year as 'making do'. Cold weather arrangements can look wonderful. I couldn't contemplate a winter without a witch hazel for character and perfume, or the scarlet leaves of *Leucothoe* 'Scarletta' to provide a colourful backdrop to winter berries and the dainty flowers of snowdrops, aconites and *Cyclamen coum*.

MUST-HAVE PLANTS FOR AUTUMN AND WINTER

Acer palmatum
 'Bloodgood'
Chrysanthemum
 'Lynn'
Crocus 'Pickwick'
Cyclamen coum
Erica carnea
Erica x *darleyensis*
Euonymus fortunei
 'Emerald 'n' Gold'
Fatsia japonica
Hamamelis x
 intermedia 'Pallida'
Hedera colchica
 'Dentata Variegata'

Leucothoe 'Scarletta'
Leucothoe fontanesiana
 'Rainbow'
Ophiopogon planis
 capus 'Nigrescens'
Ornamental
 cabbage and kale
Phormium 'Jester'
Rudbeckia hirta
 'Sonora'
Skimmia japonica
 'Rubella' and subsp.
 reevesiana
Thuja occidentalis
 'Rheingold'

Autumn window box

Slip a wooden 'jacket' over your plastic window box to give it designer style. Come winter, a change of jacket colour and a few new plants is all you need for a totally fresh look.

Plastic window boxes won't do much for your lush and attractive autumn displays, but design-style window boxes can be expensive. My answer is to hide an inexpensive plastic container inside a quick-to-make wooden 'jacket' that slips easily over the trough, and it's really easy to make – even without Tommy's skills! If you decide to place your window box on the sill of an upstairs room, it's best to get an expert to secure it firmly in place.

Start in autumn by planting your container with a long-lasting planting scheme; the one I used here contains skimmia, heuchera and ivy. The seasonal accent plants, heather and chrysanthemum, can be slipped into the display in their pots. This makes them easy to remove when you want to change the look for winter and you won't disturb the roots of the resident plants when swapping them.

When you change your planting scheme during the year you can also paint the wooden jacket a new colour to match, or paint the two long sides different colours, then all you have to do is turn it round!

WHEN TO PLANT – autumn

Making the 'jacket'

This wooden window box 'jacket' is bottomless so it can be easily slipped over a plastic container. It not only hides the trough, but helps to insulate the plants against the cold. Any timber will do, but you must seal it from the elements or it will rot. Most garden paints will do the job, but if you're unsure, give it a couple of coats of varnish inside and out.

Making the template

The template for the side panels is easy to draw on brown paper, but the template for the curved edge panels is a little more difficult. If you're confident drawing curves, draw the template freehand on paper following the guide below – if not, trace the template then enlarge it by 800%. Many newsagents have photocopiers that will enlarge to 200%. Enlarge the original by this much and then take the new copy and enlarge it again by 200%. Repeat the process one more time to get a template 800% bigger than the original. Your final copy won't fit on one A3 sheet, so you'll need to copy each end separately and tape the two pieces together.

YOU WILL NEED

Materials and tools
- Brown paper, pencil and scissors
- Timber – 2.5m x 250mm x 25mm
- Workbench or table
- 'G' clamps
- Jigsaw
- Corner clamp
- Bradawl
- 8 x 38mm corner braces
- 16 screws and screwdriver
- 4 x wooden mouldings
- Wood glue
- Garden paints in purple and green
- 800mm long plastic window box
- Chunks of broken polystyrene
- Multipurpose potting compost
- Plants (see page 106)

Charlie says…

If your windowsill is too narrow to take a window box, you can extend it quite easily. First, fix two sturdy metal wall brackets under the window. Then lay a couple of wooden strips across the brackets and screw them to the brackets. Position the window box on top.

1 *For the first curved edge panel, lay the template on the timber, aligning the bottom edge with the edge of the wood. Draw around the template, flipping it over for the other side (see diagram).*

2 *Secure the panels to the workbench with 'G' clamps. Cut the shape with the jigsaw. Make the second curved panel in the same way. Use the side panel template to draw the two side panels, then cut them out.*

3 *Use a corner clamp to clamp a side panel to a curved panel, with the bottom edges aligned and the side slightly recessed. Make starter holes with a bradawl then screw in two corner braces.*

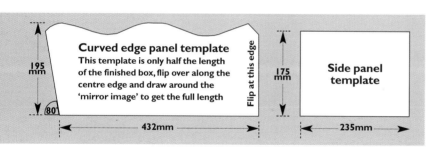

Curved edge panel template
This template is only half the length of the finished box, flip over along the centre edge and draw around the 'mirror image' to get the full length

195 mm

80°

432mm

Flip at this edge

Side panel template

175 mm

235mm

4 *Join on the remaining sides in the same way. Then lay the jacket on its back and glue two mouldings to the front. When the glue has set, turn the jacket over and glue two to the other side.*

5 *Paint one curved edge panel and both side panels purple (for autumn), and the other curved edge panel green (for winter). For good coverage you'll need two to three coats. Allow to dry between coats.*

6 *Put the plastic window box on your sill and slip the jacket over it. Place a layer of crocks in the bottom, then plant the permanent plants and put in the autumn accent plants in their pots. Water well.*

Seasonal change

When the first frosts hit, the chrysanthemums will be past their best. Heathers are slightly hardier but they, too, will soon start to fade. Replace the heathers with a red-berried evergreen *Skimmia japonica* subsp. *reevesiana* and the chrysanthemums with winter-flowering pansies and *Cyclamen* Miracle Series. These little flowers will bring colour to an otherwise all-foliage arrangement. Don't worry if your windowsill is a bit shaded because all the plants I've chosen will cope with all but the deepest shade. A word of warning for those with children, the *Skimmia* does have poisonous berries so if you include it, make sure the container is out of their reach.

FLOWERS AND BERRIES FOR WINTER

Autumn selection

The permanent plants in this display – the ivy, skimmia and heuchera – are all fairly tolerant of weather and environmental conditions and will form a solid basis for any seasonal planting. Weather conditions will determine when you replace your autumn accent plants with those for winter. You'll know when it's time to replant – the leaves of chrysanthemums will start to wilt and stems of heathers begin to dry out. Heathers are a touch hardier than chyrsanthemums and will last a bit longer. If left to dry out slowly heathers make pretty dried flowers. Before they're over, bring them indoors and plant in a decorative bowl but don't water, just leave them to dry and they will retain their colour. A squirt of hairspray will stop the flowers dropping.

English variegated ivy
(*Hedera helix* 'Eva')
This fully hardy, self-clinging, climbing or trailing variegated ivy has grey-green leaves with creamy margins all year round. If it gets too straggly, just trim off the ends.

Skimmia
(*Skimmia japonica* 'Rubella')
With dense evergreen foliage, this tough plant bears spikes of red flower buds in autumn and winter. In spring they form fragrant clusters of white flowers.

Heuchera
(*Heuchera* 'Chocolate Ruffles')
The brown ruffled leaves of this hardy perennial are burgundy underneath. It colours up best in sun but is happy in partial shade.

AFTERCARE

Don't overdo the watering – once a fortnight is usually enough. Waterlogged roots will rot or freeze.

If the permanent plants outgrow their spaces, give them a gentle trim in late spring to keep them in check or replace them with smaller plants.

Cyclamen won't flower the second year unless you rest them over the summer in the garden somewhere warm and dry. The heuchera will also benefit from a rest.

Heather or heath
(*Erica gracilis* 'Red')
This neat shrub has needle-like mid green leaves and delicate clusters of vibrant cerise, bell-shaped flowers in autumn. It grows to about 50cm (20in) tall.

***Chrysanthemum* 'Carnival Bicolour' and 'Carnival White'**
A compact plant, this chrysanthemum grows to 45cm (20in) and has masses of petals with a yellow centre in autumn. Deadhead regularly to extend flowering.

Clever wire containers

After the shout-it-out shades of summer bedding, enjoy the subtlety of plants with more muted hues. Set them off with the frosted glint of metal wire containers.

Galvanized wire containers look fabulous planted up, especially if you have a group of them. You'll find them on sale in all major department stores and in many large garden centres. But if, like me, you're into recycling, dig around the kitchen or garden shed and you'll probably find a container or two that would enjoy a new lease of life. If nothing takes your fancy, head off for the junk shops. I love wandering around them and I usually find really unusual metal containers at very reasonable prices. And if they are a little bent and battered, it all adds to the character!

The plantings I designed here echo the muted umbers, oranges and reds of the changing leaves. For containers I've used a wire wastepaper basket (back left), an egg basket (back right) and a garden trug (foreground).

WHEN TO PLANT – **from early autumn**

Preparing and planting wire baskets

These steps show you how to prepare and plant up the viola-filled wire wastepaper basket. All the wire containers should be prepared in the same way; the individual plantings are described on page 110. Galvanized wire baskets already have a rustproof coating, which makes them ideal as containers. If your basket is ungalvanized, give it a couple of coats of varnish.

Compost and fertilizer

If you want your baskets to last for more than one season, it is worth investing in a soil-based compost. It will supply your plants with all the nutrients they need. If you're worried about weight (soil-based composts are heavy) and cost, use multipurpose compost, but boost the goodness levels with slow-release fertilizer. This fertilizer breaks down in moist, warm conditions but remains in the compost for some time after it becomes inactive. Don't forget you used it and later panic if you find the empty granules in the compost and mistake them for pest eggs.

YOU WILL NEED

Materials and tools
- Old newspapers
- Galvanized wire paper basket
- Spray varnish (optional)
- Coco fibre 'moss' liner
- Water-based silver spray paint
- Black plastic bag
- Scissors
- Soil-based compost or multipurpose potting compost plus slow-release fertilizer
- Gravel (optional)

Plants
- *Viola* 'Sorbet Series' (enough plants to cover sides of basket)
- 1 x *Hebe* 'Jannas Blue'
- 1 x *Ajania pacifica*
- 1 x silverbush (*Convolvulus cneorum*)
- 1 x feather grass (*Stipa tenuifolia*)

1 *Lay old newspapers out to cover your worktable. If your container isn't galvanized, you'll need to protect it from the elements or it will rust. Spray with two coats of varnish, leaving it to dry between coats.*

2 *Lightly spray the coco fibre with the paint, allowing some green to show through. Leave to dry. This will only take a few minutes because the coco fibre is really absorbent. Line the basket with the coco fibre, painted side facing outwards.*

4 *Put a black plastic bag in the basket and trim it to just below the top of the basket. Make a few slits in the base of the bag for drainage. Put some gravel in the bottom of the liner and then add about 5cm (2in) of compost.*

5 *Spread the basket wires and cut through the coco fibre and plastic bag. Feed the viola roots through the gap into the compost, keeping the leaves on the outside of the basket. Add more compost as you plant up the sides of the basket.*

3 Mix the slow-release fertilizer through the compost at the rate recommended by the manufacturers on the packet. The active ingredients in the fertilizer should be sufficient for about one growing season.

6 Plant the rest of the plants (but not the grass) around the rim of the container. Add more compost and firm down. Finally, plant the grass in its central position and top up with compost. Water thoroughly.

Get ready for spring

After planting your autumn wire baskets, prepare a few more that look good in winter and will surprise you as they peak in spring. This second-hand basket is lined with sphagnum moss, filled with soil-based potting compost and planted with hyacinth bulbs (*Hyacinthus* 'Woodstock'), a silver-leaved cineraria (*Senecio cineraria*) and *Viola* 'Blackjack'. A good choice for winter containers, the evergreen *Senecio cineraria* has soft felty grey leaves that make a pretty carpet for any spring planting. Violas will produce lots of flowers during mild weeks throughout autumn and winter and come into full flower in spring as the bulbs appear.

PLANTED IN MID AUTUMN, THIS BASKET OF HYACINTHS, CINERARIA AND VIOLAS WILL PEAK IN EARLY TO MID SPRING

Wireworks plantings

Most of the plants selected for the wastepaper basket have been chosen for their foliage interest. All of them should be readily available from good garden centres. However, don't worry if you can't find the exact match. Simply note the general shape and colour of a plant, then find another plant with a similar look. In addition to the plants shown here, *Ajania pacifica* makes an appearance in the top of the basket. Its decorative, silver-margined leaves look good all year round and it bears small yellow flowerheads in autumn.

More plantings

For the full effect of the grouping on page 107, add the two other wire baskets to go with the viola-smothered basket. Yellow primroses,

To boost flowers later in the season, use a tomato feed.

Don't overwater your containers during the cooler months. If the compost gets too wet your plants could rot.

You can give feather grass a good haircut in early spring, before new growth comes through.

These autumn wire baskets should look great for most of the coming year. The plants will, however, have outgrown their containers by summer and will need to be repotted.

purple-leaved bugle (*Ajuga reptans* 'Braunherz'), densely tufted sedge (*Carex flagellifera*), *Sedum spurium* 'Dragon's Blood', and autumn fern (*Dryopteris erythrosora*) line the trug,

Hebe 'Jannas Blue'
A small, pretty plant with thyme-like, waxy blue-green leaves, this hebe grows into a dense mound. Its pale lilac-blue flowers bloom in late spring.

Silverbush
(*Convolvulus cneorum*)
Forming a dense, silvery-grey foliage, this silverbush gives year-round interest. It bears white, trumpet-shaped flowers from early summer.

and yellow violas, variegated ivy, green and cream striped sedge (*Carex morrowii* 'Fisher's Form'), and bellflower (*Campanula garganica* 'Dickson's Gold') the egg basket.

Viola 'Sorbet Series'
The flowers of this range of violas are very hardy and can bloom right through winter and spring into early summer. They come in yellows, blues and mauves.

Feather grass
(*Stipa tenuifolia*)
Feather grass forms a dense, grassy clump, topped in mid summer by fluffy plumes that change from beige to white. It flowers mid summer.

Winter and spring basket

Here's a clever, long-lasting container planting that combines winter-interest plants and spring-flowering bulbs, giving about six months of colour and interest.

The central foliage plant in this arrangement is the shrubby winter-flowering *Viburnum tinus*. This is partnered by white winter-flowering heathers and variegated ivies, all of which help to soften the edge of the basket. The eye-catching focus for the autumn season is the miniature cyclamen with its marbled foliage and dainty nodding flowers. The milder the winter, the longer and better these gorgeous little blooms will flower.

By spring, the arrangement is transformed. The viburnum and heathers are in full bloom, and are joined by the early dwarf daffodils and pure white crocuses. Slightly later in the season, more daffodils follow, so your wicker basket looks good for months on end.

WHEN TO PLANT – **autumn**

Planting the basket

You can use any frost-resistant container for this winter and spring display, but a wicker basket looks especially attractive in winter when there aren't many trailing plants about to hide a less perfect pot. A large wicker basket can be hung up or placed on an outside wall, table or rustic chair.

If you want to use a wicker basket for the display, buy one that is being sold to be used as a hanging basket and is pre-lined with plastic. If you can't find one, use an ordinary wicker basket and apply three coats of yacht varnish, inside and out, to protect it. Each coat will take several hours to dry completely. When the

varnish is dry, line your basket with plastic – a black bin liner is ideal.

Once the basket is planted up, hang it in a sunny sheltered spot, or

sit it raised above the ground in a similar site. Somewhere visible from indoors is ideal, so you can enjoy the long-lasting and changing display.

1   *Cut three or four 2.5cm (1in) slits in the plastic lining in the base of the basket so that excess moisture will be able to escape. Cover the base of the lining with about 5cm (2in) small polystyrene chunks, then add 5cm (2in) of compost.*

2   *Plant the viburnum at the centre back with the rootball top about 2.5cm (1in) below the basket rim. Put in the daffodil bulbs, leaving planting gaps for the groups of ivies and heathers at the centre front and on either side.*

YOU WILL NEED

Materials
- Wicker hanging basket, 40cm (16in) in diameter and plastic liner, if not lined
- Chunks of broken polystyrene
- Soil-based compost or multipurpose compost plus grit

Plants
- 1 x viburnum (*Viburnum tinus*)
- 2 x heathers (*Erica x darleyensis* 'White Perfection')
- 3 x ivies (*Hedera helix* 'Kolibri')
- 20 x dwarf daffodil bulbs (10 each of *Narcissus* 'Topolino' and *Narcissus* 'Quince')
- 10 x crocus corms (*Crocus vernus* 'Jeanne d'Arc')
- 3 x cyclamens ('Miniature F1 Miracle White')

3   *Add the ivies and heathers, and more potting compost, bringing the level to 2.5cm (1in) below the rim. Then plant the crocus corms between the plants and around the edge of your container, about 5cm (2in) below the soil surface.*

4   *Add the three cyclamens between the ivy and heather groups. Firm in the plants and water well. Put the basket in the position you've chosen for it. It is heavy, so check that the hook is secure if it is hanging up.*

Charlie says...

Bulbs to be grown in containers should be planted in autumn in a gritty, well-drained soil-based compost. If you're using a multipurpose compost, add extra grit.

Cyclamen in pots will withstand a bit of frost, but severe conditions can prove fatal unless given some protection. After flowering, the cyclamen in this basket can be left in place or removed to make way for the spring bulb shoots.

AFTERCARE

Check your basket display regularly to make sure the container compost is moist, and water if necessary. Take particular care during early spring when temperatures rise and growth is rapid.

Never water this container display if frost threatens. If freezing temperatures last for prolonged periods in winter, put the wicker basket in a garage or porch to protect the plants.

If the cyclamens are harmed by frosts, simply remove them from the display and fill in the gaps with some extra compost.

After flowering, plant the bulbs – crocuses and daffodils – in the garden. The foliage plants can be left in place ready for a new display the following year – just apply liquid feed at the end of March and again in early April.

The basket in spring

By spring, the hanging basket will be packed with flowers. The viburnum and heathers are in full bloom and the bulbs have grown. *Narcissus* 'Topolino' is a delightful dwarf daffodil with creamy petals. The goblet-shaped crocus flowers are pure white, opening in sunshine to reveal bright orange stamens. A week or so later *Narcissus* 'Quince' will come into flower with its gorgeous miniature yellow trumpets.

THE SPRING-FLOWERING BULBS GIVE THE BASKET A NEW LEASE OF LIFE WHEN THE CYCLAMENS ARE OVER

Winter and spring choices

The plants shown here provide the structure of the winter display. In addition I planted daffodil and crocus bulbs that will pop up in spring. *Narcissus* 'Topolino', an early dwarf daffodil, was chosen for its delicate beauty and for its 25cm (10in) height which makes it perfect for hanging baskets. Its early spring partner, *Crocus vernus* 'Jeanne d'Arc', is a large-flowered Dutch crocus with pure white flowers that look charming against the variegated ivies and viburnum. Each of the crocus corms produce several blooms.

There's no need to follow my selections rigidly, pick plants you like from what's available at your local garden centre. Look out for a small evergreen shrub for the central plant. *Skimmia japonica* 'Rubella' is a good choice in place of viburnum (see page 106 for information on this skimmia). Surround the shrub with heathers and ivies, which are always widely available. The autumn colour comes from cyclamens, but violas or pansies are other good choices. There are lots of other small daffodils suitable for window boxes and hanging baskets. Dwarf *Narcissus* 'Tête-à-Tête' always looks good. It grows to only 15cm (6in) high, is sturdy and is easily available. Multi-headed *Narcissus* 'Jumblie' and *Narcissus* 'Pencrebar', which has scented, golden double flowers, grow a couple of centimetres taller.

Viburnum
(*Viburnum tinus*)
This is a reliable evergreen shrub. Buy a plant with plenty of buds. When they open they will reveal a dark pink tinge which later lightens to pure white as the flowers open. The shrub flowers between late winter and early spring.

Heather
(*Erica* x *darleyensis* 'White Perfection')
This is a low spreading heather which will produce flowers from late winter through to mid spring. As an alternative selection, try planting *Erica carnea* 'Springwood White' which will trail over the sides of the wicker basket.

Cyclamen
(*Cyclamen* 'F1 Miracle White')
Grown from a small tuber, this cyclamen will flower for many weeks from early autumn onwards, even tolerating mild frosts. You can buy many different colours, such as rose, salmon, scarlet and purple, all with patterns of silver marbling on the foliage. They are often deliciously scented.

Variegated ivy
(*Hedera helix* 'Kolibri')
This is a richly variegated ivy with white marbling and a distinct burgundy-red tone to the stems. *Hedera helix* 'White Knight' is similar but there are many other alternatives available, including *H. h.* 'Glacier' with its silver-grey variegations and *H. h.* 'Goldchild' which has golden margins.

Mock stone planter

A mixture of stonecrops and houseleeks looks refreshing in autumn and will continue to look good all winter, but you need to plan ahead and make your planter in spring.

Antique stone sinks look brilliant planted with alpines and other low-growing plants, but they are hard to find and expensive to buy. They are also extremely heavy. For a fraction of the cost of the real thing, you can make a lightweight fake that looks just as good. I made the lovely, rough, 'weathered' texture of this mock stone planter by adding coarse sand and peat to the mortar mix; this mixture is sometimes called 'hypertufa'. If you prefer not to use peat, ask at your local garden centre for a similar fibrous plant material as an alternative.

Stonecrops and houseleeks are naturals for a shallow planter like this because they have short roots. With so many different leaf shapes, colours and textures (you can even get hairy ones!) easily available, you'll be spoilt for choice for your planter palette.

WHEN TO PLANT – mid to late spring

Making the mock stone planter

The best time to plant stonecrops in your sink is mid to late spring when the plants are growing strongly and can settle in quickly. So you need to get your planter ready in early spring. The polystyrene box I found was originally used to transport fresh fish. It's the ideal shape and is usually available for next to nothing from your fishmonger or the fish counter at your local supermarket. Don't worry if your box is a slightly different size from mine. Mock stone planters look good in a wide range of shapes and sizes.

YOU WILL NEED

Materials and tools
- Polystyrene fish box, about 58 x 35 x 15cm (23 x 14 x 6in)
- Wide-gauge chicken wire
- Thick protective gloves
- Wire cutters
- Craft knife
- 2 offcuts of narrow hosepipe or wooden dowelling
- Mixing board for mortar and spade
- For 'hypertufa' mortar – coarse sharp sand, fine builders' sand, quick-drying cement and fine peat (or similar fibrous plant material)
- Bucket
- 2 bricks
- Pointed trowel and soft brush
- Selection of plants
- Broken pots, gravel, compost and horticultural grit for planting

Plants
- Selection of stonecrops and houseleeks (see page 118), or heathers (see opposite)

Protect your hands by wearing thick protective gloves when cutting and bending the chicken wire. Mortar mixture can irritate your skin, so use a trowel wherever possible to apply it to the wire frame. If, like me, you prefer to use your hands to mould the fiddly bits, always put on thin plastic gloves

first. Quick-drying cement may speed up the drying process too much in warm, dry weather or if the sink is in full sun; and concrete that dries too fast may crack. To prevent this, spray a mist of water over the sink daily, and keep it covered with polythene until it sets – about a week.

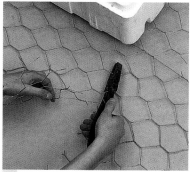

1 *Place the fish box in the centre of the chicken wire. Using wire cutters, trim away the excess wire at the corners, leaving enough to wrap up the sides and cover the entire box inside and out.*

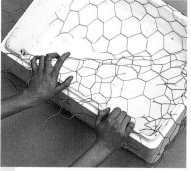

2 *Carefully mould the chicken wire around the box and into the centre of the container. The wire should closely follow the shape of the box but not be completely flush with the box surface.*

3 *Twist together any loose wire ends that are sticking out and sink these ends into the polystyrene. Polystyrene is rather delicate and breaks easily, so treat it as gently as possible.*

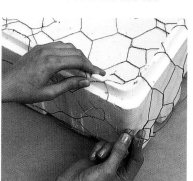

4 *Cut two small drainage holes in the bottom of the box about 23cm (9in) apart. Then push a piece of dowelling or hosepipe through each hole. The box is now ready for the mortar.*

Planting tips

Keep your eye out for a genuine antique stone sink if you're not too keen on attempting to make your own. They can be expensive, but you may get a bargain if the planter is damaged – your overflowing plants will soon cover the defects. Give an antique sink a really good clean before you start to plant it.

Move your planter to its final home when it's ready for planting. For good drainage, stand it on four bricks (one in each corner) or set it on top of gravel. The mock stone sink I made has an inside depth of about 11.5cm (4½in), which is fine for shallow-rooted plants like stonecrops, houseleeks or heather (see right). Deeper antique sinks, however, will allow you to use plants with deeper roots. Cover the drainage holes of your planter with a few crocks, then put in a thick layer of gravel. When planting stonecrops, mix plenty of coarse grit into the compost. Be sure to use a potting compost your plants will like – for instance, heathers may need a lime-free compost. Try different arrangements until the scheme looks good, then plant – filling the sink to within 4cm (1½in) of the top. A final covering of stone chippings looks good and helps to retain moisture.

A TRADITIONAL BELFAST SINK (TOP) IS A GOOD ALTERNATIVE TO THE MOCK STONE PLANTER (ABOVE), BUT CAN BE PRICEY

5 *Mix together two spadefuls each of coarse sharp sand, fine builders' sand, quick-drying cement and fine peat (or alternative) thoroughly. Slowly mix in water to make a soft, workable mortar.*

6 *Put the box on top of two bricks, then apply a 2cm (¾in) thick layer of mortar with the trowel, filling the bottom first, and curving the mortar slightly under the sides and on to the base.*

7 *Remove the pieces of dowelling or hosepipe from the drainage holes before the mortar has fully set. Brush off any surface grit with a soft brush and leave to dry completely.*

Stonecrops and houseleeks

For variety of colour and form, tough little stonecrops and houseleeks take some beating. Many stonecrops (*Sedum*) have chunky, often shiny, leaves in shades of grey, red or green. Their summer flowers are usually red, white, yellow or pink, adding to their attraction. Aside from the two sedums on this page, the planter on page 115 contains *Sedum spathulifolium*, with small rosettes of silvery grey leaves tinged with purple, and *Sedum spathulifolium* 'Capo Blanco', which is a more compact variety with all-over silver-grey rosettes that are powdery white in the centres. These are just suggestions and you can make up your own palette from whatever you can find. Not all sedums are hardy evergreens, however, so make sure you get the outdoor rockery types for your planter. Keep to the alpine section of your garden centre, and you can't go wrong. Handle stonecrops with care, as the sap can irritate the skin.

The Latin name for houseleeks is *Sempervivum* – which means 'always alive'. Houseleeks are evergreens and they can live for a long time in some inhospitable places. You will see houseleeks flourishing in shallow containers with hardly any soil. They even grow happily in cracks in walls. Poor soil is no problem for houseleeks but they do not like poor drainage or wet conditions.

AFTERCARE

Don't let one fast-growing plant swamp your planter. Cut back after flowering any plants that are getting too big.

Stonecrops require watering only in severe drought. Too much wet in winter can cause problems. If necessary, protect them from too much rain with a sheet of glass supported on bricks; this will allow air to circulate around the plants.

If you want more stonecrops, it is easy to divide them up in spring – most of them have roots on their trailing stems.

Sempervivum giuseppii
This hardy succulent is vigorous and mat-forming. The rosettes have pea-green ovate leaves that are purple-tinged at the tips. In summer red flowers appear. Grow in full sun.

Sempervivum montanum
Like all houseleeks, this one likes full sun. It has clustered open rosettes and bears red-purple flowers in summer. Give your succulents liquid feed during the growing season to encourage flowering.

Sedum acre 'Aureum'
Called 'golden wall pepper', this stonecrop has mat-forming, trailing or upright stems with bright yellow leaves. In mid summer the plant has greenish yellow star-shaped flowers. Likes full sun.

Sedum spathulifolium 'Purpureum'
Has rosettes of leaves that are mainly silvery in the centres, but the outer leaves are deep purplish red. Yellow flowers appear in summer. Plant in full sun.

Winter-flowering pot

This pretty collection of winter foliage and flowers will earn its keep from autumn when it is planted right through to the following spring.

When cold autumn weather destroys the last of your summer show of petunias, begonias and busy lizzies, it's easy to give up on your containers and spend the winter planning next summer's displays. This is a shame, because just at the time when we all need cheering up – through the cold, damp chill of winter – all you have to look at are empty pots.

I call this my winter wonder display because it's guaranteed to keep your patio pretty and your spirits high right through to early spring. You can't expect the torrent of blooms you enjoy in the summer, but this well-balanced blend of foliage, flowers, buds, berries and coloured stems is a real tonic!

WHEN TO PLANT – **late autumn or early winter**

Planting the winter pot

For even more interest and variety, it's easy to slip in a few extra little pots of dwarf winter- and spring-flowering bulbs into this arrangement. Try pot-grown snowdrops, daffodils and tulips. In a larger container, you may even find room for pots of double daisies, pansies, violas and primroses. I often find pretty varieties at my local florist.

Winter tips

Buy a container that is labelled 'frost-proof' rather than 'frost-resistant' to be sure of getting a pot that will survive the winter weather.

Good drainage for your containers is always important but it is essential in winter. Waterlogging can damage roots and cause bulbs to rot. An extra-deep drainage layer, even up to a third or half the depth of a deep pot will help. Stand the pots up on special pot feet to prevent worms from entering and blocking the drainage holes. Also, avoid composts with water-retaining gel – these are for summer.

YOU WILL NEED

Materials
- Frost-proof terracotta pot at least 40cm (16in) in diameter
- Plastic bubble wrap
- Chunks of broken polystyrene
- Multipurpose potting compost
- Garden fleece and clothes pegs (see tip on opposite page)

Plants
- 1 x Japanese cedar (*Cryptomeria japonica* 'Elegans Compacta')
- 1 x *Euonymus fortunei* 'Emerald 'n' Gold'
- 1 x *Skimmia japonica* 'Rubella'
- 2 x winter heather (*Erica x darleyensis* 'Kramer's Rote')
- 3 x pot-grown *Crocus vernus* 'Pickwick'

1 *Line the inside of your terracotta pot with plastic bubble wrap to prevent the compost from freezing and damaging the roots. Don't cover the drainage hole. Put chunks of polystyrene in for drainage.*

2 *Begin filling the pot with compost. Stop when the top of the cryptomeria rootball will sit about 2.5cm (1in) beneath the container rim – use the cryptomeria in its pot as your depth gauge.*

3 *Knock the cryptomeria out of its pot and position it at the back of your display container. Hold this little conifer steady as you raise the level of compost to suit the other plants.*

4 *Add the variegated euonymus alongside the cryptomeria, then tuck in the red-budded skimmia, leaning it out slightly over the pot rim. Fill in the front with the two winter heathers (*Erica*).*

Hellebore heaven

Charlie says…

Pack winter display pots with plants. It doesn't matter if rootballs are touching as plants make little growth in winter.

Skimmia can be damaged by really severe weather. Protect plants with a double layer of fleece wrapped round them held with clothes pegs.

Reserve one big container for a special winter plant such as witch hazel with its gloriously scented spidery flowers, or Mahonia japonica – worth growing for its foliage alone.

5 *For an extra layer of colour, add the three dwarf pot-grown striped crocus. Slip them into the gaps behind the two heathers. If they are too big to fit in, you can split them up. Firm in and water.*

A chimney pot is far too valuable a planter to waste over winter on a single specimen of trailing ivy or periwinkle. In fact, it is the ideal size and shape to show off one of winter's most sought-after plants, the Lenten rose *Helleborus orientalis*. The one I've chosen has dark purple flowers, but Lenten roses are available in shades of creams, pinks and maroons. The blooms are sometimes spotted inside, but as they hang their heads you can't see them clearly when they are planted in the ground. But raised up in a chimney pot they will greet you face to face. To contrast with the deep purple hellebore, I mixed in *Acorus gramineus* 'Ogon' with its yellow rush-like leaves and pots of early daffodils. I chose the bright yellow *Narcissus* 'Tête-à-Tête' because it's delicate, pretty and reliable.

RAISED UP IN A CHIMNEY POT PLANTER, YOUR HELLEBORES WILL GET ALL THE ATTENTION THEY DESERVE

Winter foliage and flowers

While it is always possible to plant up individual containers with just one variety – pansies in one pot, crocuses in another – the most satisfying winter containers usually have a mixture of foliage and flowers. The evergreens provide a backdrop for the more flamboyant blooms which will be the focal point of the arrangement.

Here are details about all the varieties I used in the winter wonder display, except for the *Skimmia japonica* 'Rubella' (see page 106 for information on this shrub).

AFTERCARE

Frost and wind can rob a container of moisture, so check every week that the compost is moist.

Keep your winter pot in a sunny, warm and sheltered spot.

If you 'hide' small pots of flowering plants in the display for added colour, make sure these pots get watered when you're watering the container.

When you want to free up your pot for new spring and summer displays, trim back the spent flower spikes and plant the ericas out in a bed or border. Work in some of the old potting compost around the roots. Pot up the shrubs into individual pots for future use, or plant them out in a winter-themed bed. Split up the bulbs and plant them in your garden.

Heather
(*Erica* x *darleyensis* 'Kramer's Rote')
A hybrid that will perform well in sun or shade and blooms very early, sometimes before Christmas. It is very free with its strings of hanging flowers, and makes a great carpet to show off bulbs.

Japanese cedar
(*Cryptomeria japonica* 'Elegans Compacta')
There are several conifers that go this bronze colour in winter, triggered by the cold, and this is one of the best. Its foliage is a fine backdrop for bright flowers.

Dutch crocus
(*Crocus vernus* 'Pickwick')
This attractively striped crocus is one of the large-flowered Dutch hybrids. It peaks in early spring and has sturdy, upright blooms. 'Pickwick' grows to 10-12cm (4-5in) tall.

Euonymus
(*Euonymus fortunei* 'Emerald 'n' Gold')
Tough and reliable, this dwarf yellow variegated evergreen is at its best when the new growth flushes in spring. Pick off vine weevils at night by the light of a torch. They love to nibble this plant.

Grasses and bamboos

Ornamental grasses and bamboos can live happily in containers, so take the opportunity to fill an empty corner of your garden with these stylish plants.

Ornamental grasses have been popular in Japanese gardens for a long time, but they're relative newcomers to Western garden design. For full impact, I arranged a collection of grass-like plants together in a corner of this garden. Although all the plants have the long, thin leaves characteristic of grasses, only five are true grasses –feather grass (*Stipa tenuissima*), Hakone grass (*Hakonechloa macra* 'Aureola'), and three bamboos. Of the remaining plants two are sedges, *Carex buchananii* and *Carex elata* 'Aurea', and the other is a very dark, grass-like perennial, *Ophiopogon planiscapus* 'Nigrescens'.

Plant up containers of these grasses and bamboos in late spring. To add to the oriental feel, I put a few bamboo canes of varying lengths in a tall terracotta pot, filled with shingle and topped with pebbles, and placed this in the centre of the display.

Grasses and bamboos in containers are low-maintenance and will provide interest all year round.

WHEN TO PLANT – **late spring**

Planting bamboos and grasses

When buying the plants for this display, make sure they are well established – the pots should have a few roots coming out of the bottom, but no weeds at the top.

There are many bamboos and grasses to choose from, but for the best effect, select a variety of colours and heights. For example, the bamboos used here include the 3-4m (10-13ft) tall *Phyllostachys nigra* with black canes, the 4-5m (13-16ft) tall *Phyllostachys aureosulcata* 'Aureocaulis' with dark yellow canes and bright green leaves, and the 1m (3ft) tall *Pleioblastus auricomus* with gold and green leaves. Use crocks for drainage to add weight to the pots.

YOU WILL NEED

Materials
- Assortment of 9 containers
- Broken crocks
- Multipurpose potting compost
- Slow-release fertilizer cones
- Coarse horticultural grit

Plants
- 3 x grasses – feather grass (*Stipa tenuissima*) and Hakone grass (*Hakonechloa macra* 'Aureola')
- 3 x bamboos (*Phyllostachys nigra*, *Phyllostachys aureosulcata* 'Aureocaulis', and *Pleioblastus auricomus*)
- 2 x sedges – leatherleaf sedge (*Carex buchananii*) and Bowles' golden sedge (*Carex elata* 'Aurea')
- 1 x lilyturf (*Ophiopogon planiscapus*)

1 *Water your plants well before taking them out of the pots you bought them in. Put a layer of broken crocks in the bottom of each new container. Then add a layer of potting compost.*

2 *Place each plant in its new pot making sure the top of the soil around the plant is about 3cm (1¼in) below the top of the pot. Fill in around the sides with compost.*

3 *Poke slow-release fertilizer cones into the compost and firm in. This type of fertilizer comes in various dry forms and is highly concentrated.*

4 *Add a layer of coarse horticultural grit over the top of the pot around the plant. This acts as a mulch to help the compost to retain moisture. Water well.*

DIVIDING BAMBOO

If one of the bamboos you've planted in a container gets overcrowded, take it out of its pot in spring and divide it. Taking care not to damage any stalks, use a hand saw to cut through the rootball. Repot the pieces in separate pots.

Charlie says…

When planting tall bamboos choose containers that are heavy and deep enough to keep the plant stable. Those made of terracotta or stone are ideal. Lightweight pots will not take the weight of the foliage and are easily blown over.

Many ornamental grasses are easy to grow from seed. Sow directly into a wide container or a window box, thin out after germination and watch the variety of shapes and sizes develop and flower to give a pretty and unusual display.

AFTERCARE

Keep bamboos and sedges well watered, especially when they are newly planted and after dividing. Most grasses need less water but should always be kept damp.

Trim deciduous grasses, like feather grass, back to about 5cm (2in) in the autumn to keep them tidy – fresh shoots will appear the following spring. You can tidy up evergreen grasses, such as Hakone grass, and sedges in spring by removing dead leaves. Pull out dead bamboo canes regularly to improve the look of the plant.

Displaying bamboos and grasses

The perfect site for your arrangement of grasses and bamboos is a light spot that gives some protection from cold, drying winds. This empty corner, where a tall fence meets a shed (right), provides an ideal home.

For maximum impact, arrange the plants according to heights – the tallest at the back. In this grouping of pots, the Hakone grass with its green-striped golden leaves was planted in a tall container to raise it up. You can do the same with one or two of the shorter plants you've chosen, or you can raise pots up on bricks or pedestals.

FILL A SHELTERED CORNER WITH A VARIETY OF GRASSES AND BAMBOOS (TOP RIGHT), OR KEEP IT SIMPLE WITH JUST ONE POT (BELOW) OR THREE OF THE SAME GRASS (RIGHT)

Stockists and suppliers

PLANTS

Barcham Trees plc (container trees)
Ely, Cambridgeshire
01353 720748

Bernhard's Nurseries Ltd
(trees and shrubs)
Rugby, Warwickshire
01788 521177

Capital Gardens
Alexandra Palace, London
020 8444 2555

Chapel Cottage Plants
nr March, Cambridgeshire
01354 740938

Dobbies Garden World
Lasswade, Midlothian
0131 6631941

Garden Style (specimen plants)
Farnham, Surrey
01252 735331

Ken Muir Strawberries
Clacton-on-Sea, Essex
0870 747 9111

Langley Boxwood Nursery
(box plants and topiary)
nr Liss, Hampshire
01730 894467

**Layham Garden Centre
and Nursery**
(herbaceous plants and roses)
Canterbury, Kent
01304 813267

Millbrook Garden Company
Gravesend, Kent
01474 331335

Nottcutts Garden Centres
Bagshot, Surrey
01276 472288

Paul Bromfield Aquatics (pond plants)
Hitchin, Hertfordshire
01462 457399

Smith's Nurseries Ltd
Uxbridge, Middlesex
01895 233844

The Palm Centre (palms)
Ham, Surrey
020 8255 6191

Webbs of Wychbold
Droitwich, Worcestershire
01527 860000

Wyevale Garden Centres plc
Hereford
01635 873700

POTS

B&Q (granite-style planters)
0845 609 6688

Bailey's Home and Garden
Ross-on-Wye (tin baths/buckets/troughs)
01989 563015

Brampton Willows
(willow hanging baskets)
Brampton, Suffolk
01502 575891

Capital Garden Products Ltd
Ticehurst, East Sussex
01580 201092

Ceramica de Cataluyna (garden pots)
Henley-on-Thames, Oxfordshire
01491 628994

C H Brannam Ltd
Barnstaple, North Devon
01271 343035

Iguana (chiminea)
London
020 8543 5629

Megaceramics UK Ltd
Louth, Lincolnshire
01507 601000

Pembridge Terracotta
Pembridge, Hereford
01544 388696

Pots and Pithoi (terracotta pots)
Turners Hill, West Sussex
01342 714793

Whichford Pottery (terracotta pots)
nr Shipston-on-Stour, Warwickshire
01608 684416

TOOLS AND MATERIALS

Burgon & Ball Ltd (topiary frames)
Sheffield
0114 233 8262

DEWalt (power tools)
Slough, Berkshire
01753 567055

Felco (secateurs and pruning equipment)
Leicester
0116 234 0800

J Arthur Bower's (compost)
Lincoln
01522 537561

Pots in front-cover photograph provided
by **Apta Pottery**, 01233 621090

PICTURE CREDITS

BBC Worldwide would like to thank the following for providing photographs and for permission to reproduce copyright material. While every effort has been made to trace and acknowledge all copyright holders, we would like to apologize should there have been any errors or omissions.

GE Fabbri Ltd/Susan Bell 7, **/Liz Eddison** 4, 9, 18, 21, 22, 23, 31, 32, 33, 34, 45, 67, 81, 82, 83, 84, 93, 94, 113, 123, 124, 125, **/Michelle Garrett** 4, 14, 15, 53, 54, 55, 56, 64, 65, 66, 67, 68, 73, 74, 75, 76, 77, 78, 79, 80, 104, 105, 118, **/Marie O'Hara** 8, 16, 39, 40, 41, 97, 98, 99, 100, 101, 103, 105, 106, 107, 108, 109,111, 112, 114, **/Debbie Patterson** 110, **/Lesley Rosser** 19, 71, 89, 90, 91, 92, **/Gareth**

Sambidge 25, 47, 49, 115, 116, 117, 118, **/Graham Strong** 5, 24, 27, 28, 29, 30, 35, 36, 37, 38, 43, 44, 45, 46, 50, 51, 57, 58, 59, 60, 61, 62, 63, 64, 69, 70, 71, 72, 85, 86, 87, 88, 119, 120, 121, 122

BBC Worldwide/Susan Bell 2, 12, 13, 17, 22, 24, 50, 87, 96, 100, 101, 102, 125, **/Craig Easton** 5, 117, **/John Glover** 8, 51, 52, 100, **/Tim Sandall** 6, 75, **/Richard Townshend** 11

Susan Bell 8, 9, 10, 15, 16, 20, 26, 29, 33, 37, **Liz Eddison** 48, 125, **Andrew Lawson** 76, **Ken Muir Strawberries** 96, **Clive Nichols** 80, **Debbie Patterson** 5, 13, 95, **William Shaw** 59, **Harry Smith Collection** 25, 42, **Graham Strong** 63, 121

Index

8 JUN 2002